Studies in Musical Science & Philosophy
Vol 4

The Harmony of the Spheres

Brian Capleton PhD

Adaptations from published papers

Dr Brian Capleton lectured in Piano Technology at the Royal National College, and is an alumnus of Wolfson College Oxford, the Royal College of Music, Trinity College of Music London, and Dartington College of Arts.

Published by Amarilli Books

Copyright © 2015, Brian Capleton

1st Edition

ISBN 978-0-9928141-9-9

A CIP catalogue record for this book is available
from the British Library.

This book includes material derived from
Music in Reality: The Relation of Music, Emotion and Pre-Socratic Myth
by the same author

Preface

Ideas are like plants. They grow and develop out of the soil in which they have their roots. The fully grown, mature organism may bear very little resemblance to the original seed. In this book we look carefully at the body of sources that form the earlier ground for the modern idea of *the harmony of the spheres*, and see how that has grown from its seed.

Today, of course, it is still growing. But only in certain factions. Because today, probably the majority of people have never heard of it, and we live in a world in which the mainstream understanding of the universe comes from modern science.

Modern science currently has no way of relating to ideas like *the harmony of the spheres*, other than rejecting them as incorrect, which scientifically speaking, they are. But that's because modern science, as it stands, cannot deal with the pure nature of ideas, in the first instance.

Some of the earliest extant sources for the idea of *the harmony of the spheres* which flourished for thousands of years, sources closer to the seed, show us what lies at the origins of the idea. The idea is supposed to have come from Pythagoras, and the Pythagoreans were supposed to be concerned with the relationship between Number, and the universe. But Pythagoras, despite being best remembered as a mathematician, lived in an age long before modern science.

If we are perceptive, the development of the idea of *the harmony of the spheres* from its earliest origins, highlights something about the current condition of modern science. That is, how in focusing on the nature and behavior of what exists, it completely fails to understand what nature *is*.

The idea of *the harmony of the spheres* in its original context, is very much about what nature *is*. The growth of the idea of *the harmony of the spheres* over the ages, and not least as it passes through the hands of Aristotle, is a journey that reflects a situation that we are still in today.

It is a situation in which, on the one hand, we have a growing understanding of nature through Number, in what we now call science, which today, gives rise to our technologies. But on the other hand, we are no closer, through science, to realising what nature *is*.

Today, our ideas about *the harmony of the spheres* continue to be developed from recent, previous ideas. By carefully examining the work of the earlier Greek scholars, we can see how from the very earliest times, misunderstanding arose concerning the role of Number and quantification, in descriptions of the universe.

Often, what we're told about what some earlier figure such as Pythagoras, thought about the universe, turns out to be misleading, and just part of the growth of ideas based on much earlier "misreadings" of the evidence. At the core of the transmission of the ideas, is the question of the true relationship between Number or mathematical form, and the very nature of our being.

This relationship is at the heart of the *harmony of the spheres* tradition, and it not something that science has yet answered.

Contents

The Harmony of the Spheres

The idea that humanity and the cosmos are governed by 'harmony' appears documented in Western literature two and a half thousand years ago. It is found in the writings of two pre-Socratic philosophers, Heraclitus of Ephesus (fl. BC c.500), and Empidocles of Acragas (fl. BC c.450),[1] as well as in the philosophy of Philolaus of Croton or Tarentum (fl. BC c.480), who was a Pythagorean and a contemporary of Socrates.

Heraclitus described harmony as being related to opposing tension, and he drew an analogy between Life, and the tensioned bow or lyre.[2] In Empidocles' poem *On Nature*, Love is the uniting principle and Hate the dividing principle in what is obviously a *metaphysical* cosmogony.

In his poem, those parts of creation that are alike and can be mixed, are 'united in affection by Aphrodite', whereas the 'unlike' and 'immiscible' have been 'wrought by Hate'. Nevertheless, the unlike can still be successfully mixed through the principle of *harmonia*. The poem also states that the elemental Sun, Earth, Heaven and Sea are all connected in harmony with their own parts.[3]

Most importantly, in the early sources the primary meaning of *harmonia* is usually a 'fitting together' of opposing elements rather than a specifically musical concord.[4] This *harmonia* constituted a principle of universal order[5] in a world whose many differing parts were derived from opposites created out of the originating *One*.

Opposites played an important part in early Greek thought,[6] and in Pythagorean cosmogony and cosmology, the opposites of *Limiteds*, and *the Unlimited*, appear to have been fundamental.[7] Philolaus taught that *harmonia* [8] gives order to the cosmos, and holds together the conflicting opposites of *limiters* and *unlimiteds* by attuning them.[9] Thus, in the appropriate context where unlimited possibilities of sound become limited by *harmonia*, musical harmony would be created.

The ancient tradition of the harmony of the spheres[10] is supposed to have originated with Pythagoras of Samos (fl. BC 530),[11] but the assertions within the tradition itself about its own origins, are uncertain and misleading.

The Pythagorean sect was steeped in secrecy, and the only extant Pythagorean writings that are thought to have existed before the time of Aristotle (BC 384-322) are the fragments attributed to Philolaus, and those of Archytas of Tarentum (fl. BC c.375?).[12] Furthermore, in its developed form the tradition's beguiling elements distract from the issues of real philosophical significance that surround the Myth and its supposed point of origin.

The tradition can be broadly divided into two notions. Firstly, there is the notion that actual 'sound' is produced from the movement of the celestial bodies, whether they be considered as the visible independently moving bodies, or as objects 'inherent in' celestial spheres or 'circles' from which they get their motion.

This sound was supposed to be musically harmonious, following from the fact that the principal musical intervals are governed by simple mathematical ratios. It was believed that those mathematical 'harmonic ratios' existed in the quantified positions and motions of the celestial bodies, thereby determining that the sound produced was musically harmonious.

Reports of this state of affairs in the heavens are usually accompanied by some 'rational' explanation for why the celestial sound is not audible to all. Pythagoras was believed not only to have discovered the ratios governing the principal harmonic musical intervals, but also to have had the unique and divinely ordained ability to hear the harmony of the spheres.

These beliefs in a mathematically harmonic construction of the celestial system, and sounding celestial bodies, constitute what I shall call the 'pseudo-scientific' notion and the 'quantitative' tradition.

Alternatively, in the 'metaphysical' tradition, harmony or *harmonia* is generally held to be a cosmic, Divine, and originating principle, that broadly speaking is inherent in the visible heavens, the 'soul of the world', the individual human soul, and the phenomena presented to the senses.

This notion does not necessarily demand that there be actual *sound* arising from the celestial bodies, and later in the tradition even accommodates the scientific necessity for describing the motions of the celestial bodies in more complex ways.

The metaphysical notion is in essence, a specifically musical branch of a metaphysical cosmogony in which there is an originating one-ness or Unity of all things, and in which the principle of *harmonia*, operating at all levels, combines or 'fits together' the separate parts of the created, but divided universe. In this notion, the relationship between the harmony of the heavens and earthly music, is primarily one of *kinship*, recognisable in a very special context.

That context is one in which there is *correspondence* between "Man the microcosm", and the macrocosm of the physical universe. The ability of the human soul to respond to earthly music arises from the correspondence between the nature of the soul and the nature of musical phenomena, both being Divinely ordained, and ordered through the universal principle of harmony, or *harmonia*.

Alternatively, the harmony of the spheres is taken to be something divine, that is normally only perceived by the soul before its imprisonment in the body. The soul's response to music is then seen as a 'turning to its source', and away from the body in which it is entombed.[13]

In these metaphysical pictures, mathematical order seems to indicate the presence of the metaphysical principle of harmony or *harmonia*. The relationship between the mathematical order that governs harmonic musical intervals, and their subjective musical effect, is evidence of the underlying kinship and correspondence between all things.

The correspondence, in this sense, between the nature of the soul and the nature of music, arises only because both have an allegiance to the one divine principle of harmony, or *harmonia*. Iamblichus, for example, denied that the soul actually consists of harmony and rhythm, and stated that

'the soul, before she gave herself to the body, was an auditor of divine harmony; and hence, when she proceeded into the body and heard melodies of such kind as especially preserve the divine vestige of harmony, she embraced these, from the recollected divine harmony, and tends and is allied to it, and as much as possible participates of it'.[14]

These two notions, the pseudo-scientific and the metaphysical, are not necessarily separated in any source. In Boethius, for example, the two are present simultaneously. Boethius appears to have believed in both the physical sound of the 'harmony of the spheres', and an underlying metaphysical kinship between microcosm and macrocosm, based upon harmony.

The harmony of the spheres is a notion that in totality includes both metaphysical and physical notions and embraces the mythical, the mystical, the magical, and the proto-scientific. Its true philosophical status cannot be appreciated merely in the context of only one of these.

On the contrary, the relationship between the mythical, mystical, magical, and scientific, or between the metaphysical and the physical, are themselves important questions for which the idea of *harmonia mundi* stands as a timeless monument.

The harmony of the spheres is also a notion that connects the realm of quantitative astronomy and scientific endeavour, with the essentially metaphysical endeavour of musical art. We shall begin by examining some of the evidence for *harmonia mundi* as a quantitative, astronomical proposition, and shall then move to the metaphysical aspect.

The first, and perhaps most articulate[15] description of the harmony of the spheres, in which the musical and astronomical components of the tradition appear fully developed,[16] is in Plato's account of the 'Myth of Er' in the tenth book of *The Republic*.[17]

The notion of quantifiable musical proportion in the order of the cosmos is again implicated in Plato's description of the creation of the 'world soul' in *Timaeus*.[18] The latter is the main source of the tradition's mathematical impetus, and although in it Plato describes harmonic proportions mathematically, he makes in it no *explicit* reference to music or *musical* harmony. Further allusions to cosmic music appear in *Phaedrus*,[19] and *Laws*.[20]

The description in *The Republic* takes form within a story recounted by Socrates, about the Pamphylian warrior Er, son of Armenius, who was killed in battle, but was miraculously brought back to life on the funeral pyre, after witnessing the events in the death-world.

Er was prevented from completing the death process which for the other souls ended in their reincarnation into a life of their own choosing. Unlike the other souls, he did not forget what he had seen in the 'other world', since he alone was forbidden to 'drink from the waters of the River of Lethe', the River of Forgetfulness.

In brief form, and avoiding some of the more ambiguous or contentious aspects of Plato's description, the elements of the myth most closely surrounding the harmony of the spheres are:[21]

- A rainbow-like shaft of light that bonds together the whole circumference or revolution of the heaven;[22]

- The 'Spindle of Necessity',[23] like the simple spindle used for hand-spinning on earth;[24]

- The whorl or flywheel at the lower end of the spindle which in this case is composed of eight nested 'hollowed-out' whorls of diminishing size, which are hemispherical and fitted concentrically inside one another like a nest of bowls. From the largest to the smallest they are numbered 1 to 8. Their visible rims form a continuous surface of concentric circles, and are of varying breadth. The whole spindle revolves with the same motion, but the inner seven circles revolve slowly in the opposite direction, at various speeds;[25]

- The 'lap of Necessity'[26] in which the spindle turns;

- Eight Sirens,[27] each of which stands on the top rim or circle of an individual whorl, being carried round with it, and singing a single note,[28] the eight together composing a single harmony.[29]

- Three enthroned Fates, the Moirae,[30] daughters of Necessity, Lachesis, Clotho, and Atropos, all in white, and garlanded,[31] who sit round about at equal distances[32] singing to the Sirens' harmony.[33] Lachesis sings of things past, Clotho of things present, and Atropos of things to come. The three Fates turn the whorls, Clotho from time to time turning the outermost rim with her right hand, Atropos turning the inner rims with her left hand, and Lachesis turning the inner and outer rims alternately with her left and right hands.

- The confirming of destiny, in which Lachesis provides new lives and Guardian spirits[34] that the souls themselves choose on the strength of their own virtue and ignorance; Clotho ratifies the choice by taking it into the revolution of the spindle beneath her hand; and Atropos spins the thread of destiny or life, making it irreversible.

I have so far not mentioned the further details Plato gives suggesting the geometrical arrangement of the light and the heavens, or the details concerning eight whorls, linking them by allusion to the celestial bodies and their orbits.

These details, together with those Plato gives in *Timaeus* regarding the construction of the 'world-soul', have long been plundered and compared, in numerous attempts to reconstruct an original Platonic or Pythagorean astronomical system that embodies a quantifiable celestial harmony.[35] A conclusive interpretation along these lines has been prevented by the fact that Plato's descriptions, and sometimes the Greek itself, are simply too ambiguous.

A purely quasi-scientific attempt to reconstruct a Platonic system of musico-astronomy from Plato's myths will tend to extract the mathematical and astronomical elements and treat them in relative isolation, and to ignore the import of qualitative symbols like 'the lap of Necessity', or the colour of the Fates' attire.

Yet the story is actually a spiritual and moral myth about the meaning of life and death, and not merely a parable symbolising a proto-scientific system of astronomy. The details I have given so far deliberately portray the metaphysical, rather than the pseudo-scientific context of the Sirens' music.

It should be noted that the music is not *in this context* an incidental factor, any more, say, than is the fact that the Fates are the 'daughters of Necessity'. It is integral to the myth both through its association with the whorls, and through the Fates themselves who sing to the sirens' harmony and spin the irreversible threads of fate with the spindle of Necessity.

The musical part of the myth is nevertheless all too often treated as if it were a separate, added dimension, woven into the fabric of the myth, exclusively representing some quantitative Pythagorean doctrine about harmonic arithmetic proportion in what we now call the solar system.

The astronomical details in isolation, as given by Plato, are as follows. The associations with the celestial bodies are a generally agreed point of interpretation, rather than anything explicitly stated by Plato, and it is similarly assumed that the celestial system is geocentric:

- 1st whorl: Outermost. Broadest rim. Many-coloured, spangled[36] or sparkling.[37] Associated with the sphere of fixed stars.

- 2nd whorl: 8th broadest rim. Fifth in speed. Similar to 5th whorl and yellowish. Associated with Saturn.

- 3rd whorl: 7th broadest rim. Fourth in speed. The whitest. Associated with Jupiter.

- 4th whorl: 3rd broadest rim. Third in speed, appearing to move with a counter-revolution. Reddish. Associated with Mars.

- 5th whorl: 6th broadest rim. Second fastest speed. Similar to 2nd whorl and yellowish. Associated with Mercury.

- 6th whorl: 2nd broadest rim. Second fastest speed. Second in whiteness. Associated with Venus.

- 7th whorl: 5th broadest rim. Second fastest speed. The brightest. Associated with the Sun.

- 8th whorl: 4th broadest rim. Innermost and fastest. Illuminated by the seventh from which it takes its colour. Associated with the Moon.

In *Timaeus* Plato tells how God constructed the soul of the world out of three constituents, forming what from his description appears to be something like an armillary sphere.[38] We will not here closely scrutinise the details Plato gives, other than to say that the process involves dividing something called 'the whole' into proportions determined by the series of numbers 1, 2, 3, 4, 8, 9 and 27.

These numbers are used in the discourse to produce 'intervals'[39] in the harmonic proportions 2/1, 3/2, 4/3, 9/8, and 256/243, which correspond to the octave, fifth, fourth, whole tone,[40] and diatonic semitone of the old Pythagorean tuning.[41]

This correspondence, however, is circumstantial as it appears in the text, and Plato makes no explicit reference to musical harmony. Cornford argued that the series was employed for reasons that have nothing to do with music.[42] Plato also describes 'circles' being made, whose motions correlate to the motions of the whorls in the Myth of Er.

The quantitative, physical idea behind the general form of the *harmonia mundi* concept as it appears in the later pseudo-scientific tradition is not dependent upon the metaphysical or mythical notion of singing Sirens or Moirae, but prosaically assumes that the celestial bodies, being large and fast-moving, must produce from their movements sounds whose pitches are associated with their size, speed, and position.

This branch of the tradition held that the bodies move at speeds which are related to their distances from the centre of the system, generally with the slower moving bodies giving the lowest notes, and the fastest moving, the highest notes.

In a further extension of this pseudo-scientific hypothesis, the radii of the orbits and the sidereal speeds of the celestial bodies are said to be somehow arithmetically arranged in harmonic proportions with the result that the sounds produced are musically harmonious, or correspond to a musical harmony or scale.[43]

This sound was sometimes said to have been audible to Pythagoras, but not audible to everyone because from birth everyone was exposed to it, and in the absence of genuine, contrasting silence, everyone was adapted and unaware of it.

An Unlikely Story

It is Plato's pupil, Aristotle - assumed to have been the earliest important authority on the Pythagoreans[44] - who provides in his *De Caelo* the first explicit exposition of this pseudo-scientific account,[45] and he does so with the intention of disputing it. Aristotle also purported to give metaphysical legitimacy to the notion of concentric celestial spheres.

The concept of concentric spheres in the heavens had appeared much earlier, in the philosophy of Anaximander (BC c.610-546), and had later been developed by Eudoxus (BC c.390-340), who proposed a system 26 spheres as a mathematical model intended to explain the combined motions of the stars and planets.[46]

Eudoxus envisaged each inner sphere revolving on an axis attached to the surrounding sphere, the system thereby allowing complex motion. Eudoxus' pupil Callipus (BC c. 370-c.300) improved the scheme by adding a further eight spheres.[47]

Aristotle then brought the conjectured number up to 54, but for Aristotle concentric celestial spheres are also important as an essential part of his own system of 'metaphysics'. They are composed of 'eternal substance', 'immovable in itself', but which itself moves the planets and stars, since they are incapable of moving by themselves.[48]

The celestial bodies were, Aristotle maintained, 'fastened to' or 'inherent in' the spheres that move them,[49] an idea confirmed by Theon of Smyrna and attributed to Pythagoras himself.[50] The inability of the celestial bodies to move by themselves, and their attachment to, or inherence in the spheres, was seen by Aristotle as a significant factor in demolishing the doctrine of the harmony of the spheres.

The celestial bodies could not produce sound, Aristotle argued, since there was no relative motion, friction, or concussion. He argues that

'A thing moving in something which is not moved makes a sound; but a thing moving in something which moves continuously and causes no concussion, cannot possibly make a sound'.[51]

Aristotle thus rejected the pseudo-scientific doctrine as he understood and described it. In *Metaphysics* he repudiated the whole idea of cosmic harmony based upon number,[52] and considered that the Pythagoreans had engaged in the spurious adaptation of 'numbers and harmonies' to the 'properties and parts of the heaven and its whole arrangement'.[53]

Alexander confirmed Aristotle's position in his commentary on Aristotle's *Metaphysics*,[54] just as countless others must have rejected the idea since. But how authoritative was Aristotle's account in the first instance?

Aristotle himself speaks of, but does not disclose the alleged quantified Pythagorean scheme defining a relationship between musical intervals and an astronomical system. According to Alexander, who also offers no quantified Pythagorean scheme but instead invents his own example.[55]

Aristotle knew no details of Pythagorean cosmic harmony.[56] If so, was Aristotle merely reiterating an existing belief, perhaps widely held, but nonetheless based only upon ignorance and impression? The secrecy surrounding the early Pythagorean school would scarcely make it unreasonable to draw this conclusion.

Iamblichus (250-325 AD) noted that there were very few Pythagoreans whose writings were then known, and said that 'their excellence in keeping secrets provokes admiration'.[57] Admittedly, Iamblichus does also mention three books published by Philolaus, a member of the Pythagorean fellowship. These were said to have been bought by Dion of Syracuse, on Plato's advice.[58]

The story thus infers that as Plato's pupil, Aristotle may possibly have seen a written, quantitative exposition of Pythagorean doctrine, if indeed such a doctrine existed. If we take Philolaus' birth to have been BC c.480, then Philolaus would probably have been in his seventies by the time Plato was eighteen years old.

Given that we do not know when Philolaus died, one *could* argue the possibility that there is some truth in the story, and that Plato himself had seen a clear exposition of a quantitative doctrine by Philolaus. However, the quantitative doctrine Aristotle alludes to is not explicated anywhere in Plato.

If we are to be pedantic, then it has to be said that if Philolaus' writings were in close circulation when Plato was a young man, it can be argued that Aristotle may have seen a written Pythagorean doctrine by Philolaus.

All this conjecture in support of Aristotle is arguably rather weak, and there still remains a glaring inconsistency within Aristotle's portrayal of the Pythagoreans. It was understood by Aristotle that in Pythagorean cosmology the Earth was not at rest,[59] but revolved around a central 'fire'.

This central 'fire' was not necessarily taken to be the visible sun, and Aristotle explicitly mentions the *motion* of the sun, in his description of the Pythagorean 'doctrine'.[60] Aristotle also understood that Pythagorean cosmology included an invisible[61] 'counter-earth', which he says was only introduced in order to make the number of celestial bodies equal ten, a number that the Pythagoreans regarded as perfect.[62]

However, including the sphere of fixed stars, a system with both the Sun and Earth orbiting a centre would have eleven and not ten celestial orbits.[63] The sphere of fixed stars was treated as an integral part of the rotating celestial system elsewhere in early Greek astronomy, and Aristotle makes no mention of the sphere of fixed stars being treated separately or differently by the Pythagoreans.

There is no reason given in his report to suggest he understood Pythagorean cosmology as excluding the sphere of fixed stars from the pseudo-scientific scheme of cosmic harmony. Burkert has stated that Nicomachus proposed a system that contradicted the reports of Aristotle, as it excluded the sphere of fixed stars and assigned the moon the highest note.[64]

It might be argued that Aristotle made a simple oversight in mentioning the *movement* of the Sun, and that he actually understood the Pythagorean system as having the stationary visible Sun as the central 'fire'. However, if that was the case, then Aristotle's understanding would still be suspect, as it would in this respect then be at variance with the attestations of both Aëtius[65] and Simplicus,[66] in the description of the Philolaus' cosmology.[67]

Aristotle's account of Pythagorean cosmology is thus questionable, and the assertion that the harmony of the spheres was a quantitative, quasi-scientific notion invented by Pythagoras - an assertion that seems to have originated with Aristotle - begins to loose some of its credibility on close examination.

In the later tradition there appear a number of systems that are attributed to Pythagoras,[68] and there seems to be no reason for ascribing absolute credibility to any one over another. The writings of the Pythagorean Philolaus do not help clarify the matter. Philolaus' astronomical system has been subject to what Huffman has described as 'the widest range of assessments imaginable'.[69]

The first detailed account that seems to be have been based upon something like Philolaus' system, is by Plutarch (c.50-c.120 AD), who contradicts Aristotle by describing the distances of the heavenly bodies from the central fire as increasing by powers of three.[70]

Huffman was sceptical about Aristotle's attestations generally, stating that 'following the work of Cherniss (1935), many other detailed studies have shown that Aristotle is very prone to reformulate earlier philosophy in his own terminology and for his own dialectical purposes'.[71]

Scepticism about the plausibility of a Pythagorean origin to the pseudo-scientific tradition is not difficult to find amongst scholars. Burkert states that a mathematical system of celestial harmony before Eudoxus is difficult to conceive, and dismisses as a misconception the view 'put forward again and again as virtually self-evident' that the notion of cosmic music was inferred from a scientific system.

He also criticises the 'scale of the music of the spheres which in later times was most widely known and attributed to Pythagoras', as a 'botched version of Eratosthenes' exposition'.[72] He argues that it is only 'in pre-scientific conceptions of order that the idea of cosmic music has its roots',[73] and that the original doctrine was not a scientific system worked out in detail, and according to the earliest testimonia was not even based on any detailed astronomical system.[74]

The other area of difficulty in alleging a Pythagorean quantitative or pseudo-scientific doctrine, concerns the mathematical ratios governing the musical intervals. The idea that it is arithmetic harmonic ratios inherent in the celestial system that are responsible for its alleged musically harmonious properties, is necessarily based upon a knowledge of the relation between musical harmony and arithmetical, harmonic proportions. The part of the tradition that ascribes to Pythagoras the discovery of the relation between the ratios 6 : 8 : 9 : 12 and the octave, fifth, fourth, and whole tone, is itself most probably spurious.

Pythagoras is said to have listened to the hammers of four smithies, which were striking the metal and ringing out notes in the musical relation of a fourth, fifth, and octave.

The story itself, as it is reported by Nicomachus, Iamblichus, and numerous others,[75] is well known to be certainly fictitious because it explicitly asserts Pythagoras to have discovered the arithmetical ratios *via* acoustical laws which we know do not exist.[76]

Levin put both the musical and astronomical parts of the tradition in perspective, emphasising that an inverse proportion exists between the quantity of extant documentation and its date of origin, and stating that 'despite the weight and centuries old persistence of the ancient tradition ascribing to Pythagoras such acoustical and astronomical discoveries as would provide a basis for the doctrine, it is impossible to discover any concrete evidence that might justify the attributions'.[77]

Levin argued against both AE Taylor[78] and Sir Thomas Heath,[79] who accepted Pythagoras as the discoverer of harmonic ratios, and refuted the view of A Delatte[80] that the ancient reports are unanimous in ascribing the discovery to Pythagoras.

JA Philip confirms Levin's view that there are no good grounds for believing Pythagoras discovered the three intervals [fourth, fifth and octave], and that it is probable that the idea of *harmonia mundi* came from connecting the seven notes and seven planets.[81] Philip suggests that the idea originated as a poetic insight.[82]

More specifically, it has been alternatively suggested that the source of the idea may have come from an association of the seven strings of the lyre with the seven planets in the geocentric celestial system.[83] According to Boethius, music 'in the beginning' was made on only four strings, and remained that way until the time of Orpheus, when more strings were added.[84]

There is a traditional belief, traceable to Nicomachus, that Pythagoras added an eighth string to the seven-string lyre, thereby creating a diatonic octave.[85] A close qualitative association of actual musical instrument strings with the astronomical system is also evident in the thought of Claudius Ptolemy.

Ptolemy is perhaps better known as a contributor to the quantitative tradition, and the originator of the geocentric celestial system that predominated for fifteen centuries until the scientific revolution,[86] but at the beginning of his extensive three-book treatise entitled *Harmonics*, he states that the student of *harmonics* must aim to preserve the idea of musical intervals, and that the astronomer must aim to preserve the model for harmonic movements of the heavenly bodies.[87]

Whether or not Pythagoras did actually discover the harmonic ratios himself, the fact is that the earliest extant occurrence of the smithy story is the one by Nicomachus,[88] and his account is described by Levin as a 'fairy-tale' version, complete with a "once upon a time" and a miraculous circumstance, that could have been derived from near Eastern myths about the origins of music'.[89]

Circumstantial Evidence

There is thus a serious lack of solid evidence supporting the traditional claim that the *quantitative* notion and tradition of *harmonia mundi* is Pythagorean in origin. So, if the quantitative notions are connected to Pythagoras only through rumour, what kind of circumstantial fire is there in pre-Socratic writing, behind the vast amount of quantitative, quasi-scientific smoke that has been produced?

The earliest attempt to quantify the dimensions of the lunar and solar orbits is found in the reported philosophy of Anaximander,[90] who was not a Pythagorean, but a member of the Ionic School. The details known are related to Anaximander's cosmogony. The cosmogony involves the formation of at least three concentric 'circles or rings' about the Earth.

These were formed when a 'sphere of flame (or fire)' that had grown around the Earth, forming certain circles.[91] These 'wheel-like' circles of fire, are enclosed by 'compressed masses of air' that have 'pipe shaped passages', 'vents', 'nozzles' or orifices, through which the fire is 'exhaled'.[92]

These form the visible sun, moon, and 'stars' [presumably including the planets], and eclipses occur when the vents are obstructed. According to Aëtius, something akin to this notion of 'air' obscuring an enclosed fire, occurred in Empidocles' cosmology, where the enclosing 'air' or 'mist' is described with an explicitly solid, crystal-like form.[93]

Anaximander's astronomical quantifications begins with the Earth, which according to the reports, he held to be 'rounded, circular, like a stone pillar', or like a cylinder, one of whose plane surfaces is that on which we stand. The depth is one third of the breath.[94]

Next, are the attestations by Hippolytus and Aëtius regarding the sun and the Earth. Hippolytus states in a corrupt passage[95] that 'the circle of the Sun is twenty-seven times as large as the earth, and that of the moon is nineteen times as large as the earth.[96]

Aëtius states:

- 'The sun is a circle twenty-eight times the size of the earth...'[97]

- 'The sun is equal to the earth and the circle from which the sun gets its vent and by which it is borne round is twenty-seven times the size of the earth.'[98]

- 'The moon is a circle nineteen times as large as the earth; it is like a chariot-wheel, the rim of which is hollow and full of fire, like the circle of the sun....'[99]

- 'The sun is placed highest of all, after it the moon, and under them the fixed stars and the planets.'[100]

The ambiguities and lack of consistency in these simultaneous statements are all too obvious.[101] As far as his cosmology is concerned, it is not clear whether Anaximander's 'stars' are formed from more than one 'circle'. If the five planets each had a sphere, then the total of eight spheres would potentially be musically significant,

28

but the extant attestations quantify only two circles and three celestial bodies.

The three obvious musically significant ratios of 2:1, 4:3, and 3:2, for the octave, fourth, and fifth, cannot be found in Anaximander's figures, and could only be generated with a great deal of inductive imagination. It must also be said, that although Anaximander's cosmogony contains quantification, it need not necessarily be interpreted as quasi-scientific in nature, particularly in respect of the spheres of flame.

It could be just as well argued that this is a mystical description expressed in physical terminology. We will look at this argument more closely, a little later. We cannot be certain one way or the other.

Next, we come to Archytas.

Huffman has suggested that Philolaus should be regarded as the primary Pythagorean source for Aristotle.[102] Philolaus would have been an important source of evidence, given that he lived about a century before Aristotle. But the contents of the fragments of Archytas, which are a Pythagorean source approximately contemporaneous with Aristotle, reveal an altogether more intriguing correlation with the assertions of Aristotle about the Pythagorean doctrine.

However, what Archytas says in the Diels fragments[103] falls significantly short of confirming Aristotle's account. Archytas begins by praising the discernment of mathematicians, saying that they have 'handed on to us a clear judgement' concerning the mathematical studies of astronomy, arithmetic, geometry and music, which he says 'appear to be related'.[104] He then says 'They are concerned with things that are related, namely the two primary forms of Being'.

Very significantly, or so it seems, he then embarks on a lengthy exposition on the physics of sound production from moving bodies. Notably, he also offers explanations as to why some sounds cannot be heard by us, saying that this can be because they are too faint, too great a distance from us, or even because they are too loud.

Next he explains why swift motion produces high-pitched sound, and slow motion, low-pitched sound, but in all of this discourse no mention is made of the celestial bodies producing sound.[105]

After this acoustical thesis, we have a short section on the mathematics of music. This speaks about the three 'means' - arithmetic, geometric, and 'harmonic' - and is no more than a statement about the arithmetic rules.[106] In the next section of discourse the attention has moved on to other matters.

Here is revealed a very pragmatic and unmystical view on the acquisition of knowledge, and this leads on to asserting the place of *right reckoning* in civil order. Lastly, a fragment said to be from a work entitled 'Conversations', states that in regard to wisdom, arithmetic seems to be far superior to all other sciences.[107]

Thus all the basic elements of the Pythagorean doctrine as alleged by Aristotle, seem to occur *in isolation* from each other in the Archytas fragments contained in Diels, but we are confronted with a number of critical 'missing links' that would be essential in order to interpret the fragments as anything other than circumstantial evidence of the quantitative doctrine.

Archytas is certainly a good witness to the importance placed upon mathematics in Pythagoreanism. He refers once to *Being*, but there is otherwise nothing mystical or mythical in what Archytas says.

Whilst with an inductive leap it could be inferred from what he says that the celestial bodies might produce harmonic sounds if their speeds were suitably related, the extant fragments contain no such actual assertions.

And what of Philolaus?

To construe the quantitative doctrine as being inherent in the fragments attributed to Philolaus, would require an even greater effort of induction. The significance of Number is mentioned, as are harmonic ratios and universal harmonia, but there is no inference that musical harmony is inherent in the heavens, either acoustically or through harmonic, arithmetical ratios.[108]

Philolaus, as we shall see later, is far more interesting for his qualitative, metaphysical notions, both in the fragments attributed to him and in the later attestations.

The *One* and *Harmonia*

What we are confronted with in the sources is a mixture of what appears to be *quantitative*, or proto- or pseudo-scientific assertions, and *qualitative* or metaphysical discourse.

The qualitative is mythical or mystical, and is couched in terms of the Divine, Being, Mind, soul, the creation of the world out of the One through opposites, and the principle of *harmonia*, binding together and ordering the opposing elements.

The quantitative appears as the discussion of mathematical or numerical principles, or as quantitative and numerical assertions. It is not immediately apparent how a division between 'mystical' or 'mythical' thought, and 'scientific' thought, is to be made; nor is it clear how the two were connected. In the sources the two strands can be intertwined in one discourse.

It has often been supposed that in Pythagoreanism a mystical significance must have been ascribed to mathematical order. Dividing the length of a musical string by certain simple whole number proportions yielded musically harmonic intervals. Surely, it is frequently argued, this was seen by Pythagoreans as evidence of the mystical power and significance of Number?

The Pythagoreans were reported by Aristotle to have claimed that 'all things are Number'. Does this not imply that Number is the Reality or substance behind the appearance of the world? Is this not the Pythagorean doctrine that makes the quantitative *harmonia mundi* so important?

This is quite a commonly encountered interpretation of Pythagoreanism, but it fails to look beneath surface appearances. The Pythagoreans placed great importance upon Number and recognised its quantitative and predictive power. They saw that certain natural physical phenomena were governed by Number. But that does not mean that the original Pythagoreanism celebrated Number as an ultimate mystical cause or 'substance' in itself.

Number can have more than one role in mystical thought, and its appearance in an ancient source is not necessarily to be taken only as an expression of what now seems like scientific, quasi-scientific, or mathematical thought. This is amply illustrated in the following outline of a dispute between the scholars Kahn and Dicks.

In *Anaximander and the origins of Greek cosmology*, CH Kahn asks if Anaximander's quantifications should be considered as part of a mythic or a scientific point of view,[109] and concludes in favour of considering Anaximander as the 'earliest known type of mathematical physicist' outside Babylonia.[110]

This view was attacked by DR Dicks in *Early Greek astronomy to Aristotle*, as a distorted picture.[111] Distorted it may or may not be, but examination of the context of Kahn's comment reveals something far more important.

What Kahn was effectively asking, was if Anaximander's use of number in his cosmology was proto-, pseudo-, or quasi-scientific, or alternatively if he had introduced numbers as a mystical or metaphysical symbol. Kahn's description of Anaximander as a 'physicist', in the modern sense of the word, was a *relative* judgement made by comparing Anaximander's use of number specifically with the role of number in an explicitly mystical source - the Indian *Vedas*.[112]

Sir Thomas Heath had previously suggested that Anaximander's three-stage cosmogony is little more than a reiteration of the three cosmic steps of *Vishnu* from Heaven to Earth.[113] Kahn's comment, the comment criticised by Dicks, was part of a negative response to Heath's assertion, a response that ran as follows.

Kahn recognised that if Anaximander's quantifications are considered as having been made for *mythical* reasons, then something is profoundly lacking in Anaximander's mythology and viewpoint, when compared with the *Vedas*, which also use quantification.

What Anaximander seems to be lacking, is clearly present and self-evident in the stature and profundity of the *Vedas*. Kahn's view is that the mythical discourse in the Rigveda cannot be reduced to mere poetry or superstition, and that there is nothing comparable in the Greek tradition, even as far back in time as Homer.[114]

Kahn goes on to illustrate that in the *Vedas*, the number 3 is significant because it symbolises the descent from One-ness or Unity, to duality, and thence to the world of plurality in general. When it is raised to the second power, the number 9, the significance is increased in the way we might enhance the meaning of "forever" by saying "forever and ever".[115]

The use of number in the *Vedas* is part of a language that is deeply metaphysical in meaning yet quantitative in form, that is used for 'expressing the grandeur and perfection of the universe considered as a whole'. In Anaximander, numbers are not used in this way, and are not symbols in a context of the Divine, but are prosaic figures relating to the diameters of concentric circles.[116]

If one reads the Anaximander attestations one sees in them nothing that compares to other qualitative, metaphysical discourses, even of other *Greek* philosophers, for example Philolaus.[117] The same thing can be said of the writings by Archytas.

What Anaximander and Archytas say, appears to be primarily proto-physics, and has very little, if anything at all, to do with overtly metaphysical cosmogony, the mystical, or the Divine. It portrays an outlook very different from that of the ancient East, and distinct from that of say, Philolaus or Empidocles, who share in a perhaps diminished way, something of the mysticism of the *Vedas*.

This suggests that although the Greek sources, in common with the *Vedas*, contain mystical or mythical prose relating to the creation of duality, and thence the world of plurality, out of the originating One, they are already in some degree removed from the depth of mystical vision inherent in the *Vedas*, and have also begun to exhibit in some cases an intellectual pre-occupation with the quantitative structure of the universe, as a *separate* branch of their concerns.

Nevertheless, both branches of concern co-exist in the sources. The only thing that could possibly *link* those otherwise separate concerns, would be a belief, taken for granted, that quantitative order is itself a manifestation of Divine order, and a manifestation of *harmonia*.

One of the hallmarks of Pythagoreanism (and of other pre-Socratics) seems to be the conjunct appearance of the mystical or mythical, with the quantitative. As we have said, many would argue that the Pythagoreans ascribed a mystical significance to *Number itself*, usually in a numerological way. But even if they did, this would not conflict with an originating philosophy that saw Number as an important manifestation of *harmonia*, *harmonia* being the first mystical principle.

Even explicit numerological mysticism need not automatically be interpreted as the belief that mathematical order in itself, *is* the Divine, the Real, or an ultimate structure or cause, rather than the working of Divinely ordained *harmonia*, fitting together and ordering the manyfold parts of a universe created through opposites, out of the One.

Thus, the Pythagorean concern with Number, can be seen as partly a quantitative, predictive order, and partly as a qualitative, mystical symbol. This does not imply that Pythagoras must have held *Number itself* to be the highest mystical reality. There is no reason why 'The One' should be seen as having been demoted from this position. 'The One is the beginning of everything' says Philolaus.[118]

Can we argue that 'the One' is itself a numerical concept? Philolaus gives us no reason to assume this, and some very good reasons to reject such an idea. In one fragment Philolaus states 'The first composite, the One, which is in the centre of the sphere, is called the Hearth'.[119] 'The Hearth' is reported in the attestations that mention it, to be the centre of the Philolaic celestial system.

If it is part of the celestial system then it is not an abstract numerical concept. It would still be safer to accept 'The One' as a metaphysical concept linked with Being, just as it is in other sources, East and West. We then have to ask the more interesting question 'how can 'The Hearth', or 'The 'One', if it is really a 'metaphysical' concept, also be a *physical* concept, with a physical position at the centre of the physical celestial system?'

An answer to this is that there is no reason why the 'One' should not be regarded as the 'Hearth' at the centre of the physical celestial system, *at the same time* as being the *metaphysical* 'origin of all', as long as the celestial system is not primarily seen as some 'Reality' in its own right, but rather, is regarded as merely a material representation, or symbol, of a more fundamental metaphysical reality.

This is actually already an idea commonly found in mystical and metaphysical thought. In this sense, the Pythagorean view of the universe would be somewhat similar to the view presented by the ancient East, and it would certainly be consistent with Plato's view.

Could it be that Philolaus perhaps merely meant that the universe *physically* came out of this originating 'One', or 'the Hearth', like planets out of a sun? Is this what he meant by saying 'The one is the beginning of everything'?

We *could* argue this if we are looking for Philolaus the scientific cosmogonist. But if we look to Philolaus the mystic we could just as easily say that the 'Hearth' is a mystical entity. Its status as the origin or beginning of physical existence is then *symbolised* by the fact that the celestial bodies revolve around it. In this way, the system of celestial bodies is not so important as a physical system, but is important in that *symbolises* the metaphysical hierarchy behind it.

Confusion at source

Even though the early Greek sources may exhibit an interest in Number and quantitative structure that is often distinct from mythical or mystical ideas, the qualitative and quantitative faces of the philosophy are not separable in any clearly defined way.

The existence or co-existence of apparently distinct kinds of discourse, for example the mixture of the proto- or pseudo-scientific, with the metaphysical, poses something of a hermeneutical problem if whole sections of discourse are not to be ignored in favour of others. 'Myth', 'philosophy', and 'science' can co-exist at source.

Generally speaking, there is understood to be a transition from Myth to 'philosophy' (from *mythos* to *logos*) that took place between the 9th and 6th centuries BC.[120] In the sixth-century BC we find Orphic mythology co-existing with Pythagoreanism, the earliest reference to Orpheus being by the poet Ibykos.[121]

The apparent duality between myth, and mathematics as represented by the Pythagoreans, is enhanced by the fact that the Pythagoreans and Orphics do not seem to have been closely associated with each other in the 5th and 4th century evidence.[122] Nevertheless, Pythagoras is thought to have regarded Orpheus as a chief patron,[123] and there is evidence that the Pythagoreans even used Orpheus as a pseudonym.[124]

Guthrie has argued that Pythagoras was 'working on a mythical background',[125] and that the Orphics and Pythagoreans shared the same concern - the generation of the many out of the One.[126] The difference is that whilst

Orphic cosmogony is mythical and expressed in terms of personal agents, marriage, and procreation, Pythagorean cosmogony was expressed in terms of numerical ratios.[127] In many respects, Guthrie argues, one is the counterpart of the other.[128]

This does not mean Pythagoras was attempting to express myth, mathematically. It means that something significant in human knowledge that finds expression through myth, later found expression in a quantitative 'language' used by Pythagoreans who had particularly noted quantitative order in the universe.

If this is so, then the original *quantitative* expression of the harmony of the spheres, *even if it existed*, may not be important other than as a philosophical symbol, either to us, or in the original context of Pythagoras' own philosophy. It may have been introduced as a piece of inductive reasoning based upon the observation that there *is* mathematical order, and hence mathematical 'harmony', between the many parts of the manifest universe.

The need to further the doctrine by describing actual sound coming from the celestial bodies, is then completely redundant *except as a further symbol* in the communication of the metaphysical philosophy behind the doctrine.

So even if the original Pythagoreans did use this kind of description, Aristotle's objection would then amount to a case of inappropriately taking a metaphorical or allegorical description literally, and predictably declaring the pseudo-scientific thesis that it may later have been taken to be, as scientifically untenable.

Let us also propose for a moment that the 'missing links' in Archytas had existed, but are now lost, and that Archytas *had* confirmed exactly what Aristotle asserted the Pythagoreans believed about the celestial bodies, in respect of them producing actual sound. Would that alter the position? I suggest not. On what basis would we be ascribing greater authority to Archytas' account than to Aristotle's?

Presumably it would be on the basis that he was himself a Pythagorean. But here we are beset with even greater uncertainties. Were all Pythagoreans perpetually in agreement with one another? Did the Pythagorean school continue to propagate the teaching of Pythagoras exactly as he had communicated it?

Do we know that even Pythagoras' closest disciple had absorbed Pythagoras' teaching without distortion? How can we be confident that the understanding of Archytas, a century and a half later, represents with any fidelity that which Pythagoras himself taught?

The only part of Pythagoreanism that would be immune or resistant to change, corruption, or misunderstanding, would be the mathematical verities or numerological assertions. The square on the hypotenuse still equals the sum of the squares on the other two sides, and the ratio associated with the perfect fifth is still 3 : 2. But what of the original metaphysical or mystical part of Pythagoreanism, as taught by Pythagoras?

Would it even have necessarily survived intact as part of Archytas' own understanding? Pupils do not generally follow their teachers blindly, indefinitely. Few are perfect disciples and most stand to develop a different outlook from their teachers, and propagate a different teaching. Plato and Aristotle are a prime example. Over a number of centuries in a changing civilisation the role of hermeneutics cannot be ignored, especially within an oral tradition.

Number as a symbol of *harmonia*

We thus have plentiful hearsay evidence, but no primary evidence for an original, quantitative, Pythagorean doctrine of the harmony of the spheres. If we do not interpret the Pythagorean emphasis on Number as an assertion that Number *is* the originating cause of everything, the Divine, or the Real, then the search for the details of an original quantitative *harmonia mundi* becomes questionable.

Number is then the manifestation of *harmonia*, which is itself not only an earlier, but a higher and more fundamental principle. Furthermore, *harmonia* can be *symbolically* represented by Number, without necessarily inferring that the thing Number relates to, is actually and measurably quantifiable.

As it turns out, this is entirely necessary, since 'the soul' is primarily a metaphysical concept. Thus the soul can be 'joined to the body through number'[129] or the 'soul of the world' or a man's soul can be proportioned numerically, as they are in Plato, without inferring that 'the soul' is physically measurable. Alternatively, where Number is used as a *metaphysical symbol*, a physical thing predicated in numerical terms, is merely a physical symbol of *harmonia*.

Just as unmeasurable, metaphysical things like *the soul* can be predicated numerically, so numerical predication in a Greek source is not necessarily an indication of a proto-scientific viewpoint, a numerological viewpoint, or a viewpoint that upholds Number as an originating cause of all things. In the Greek sources mentioned, Number may not appear to be used in the way it is in the *Vedas*, but that does not mean its use cannot be metaphysical and allegorical.

Since the use of Number can be as a metaphorical symbol rather than an assertion that metaphysical things are literally predicable in numerical terms, Plato's quantitative description of the creation of the 'world soul' in *Timaeus*, is not necessarily most important as evidence of a physical cosmology.

When it is interpreted as such, the details that appear to be quantifying the celestial system, may assume a proto-scientific importance that is irrelevant to the more important metaphysical message they are being used to convey. And yet it has been repeatedly plundered and analysed for evidence of 'Plato's mathematical system', even in the face of the fact that Plato is recognised as what philosophers call an *idealist*, and hence, fundamentally, a metaphysician! Plato's metaphysics is not a philosophy in which *harmonia* is an effect of Number.

Number may have been held by the Pythagorean Philolaus to be essential or even a prerequisite to physical existence, but even this does not mean that *harmonia* has to be *originated* by Number. We must also not forget that, as I have said, in a metaphysical cosmogony or cosmology, physical existence is often held to be secondary to the metaphysical reality behind it. *Harmonia* itself would be a metaphysical thing, behind the scenes of existence, as it were.

Only through Number can physical multiplicity actually exist, so it would not be surprising to find Number as the essential ordering power of a physical existence whose nature is multiplicity. In this way, Number is always present

42

as the servant, symbol, and reflector of *harmonia*. Just as the physical arrangement of the universe can *symbolise* the metaphysical reality behind it, so too, can the apparently autonomous laws of Number.

The laws of Number are actually what Wittgenstein called *logical form* in action. The *logical form* of Number is the *logical form* of the physical universe, or *vice versa*. The *logical form* is something that *shows* *itself* in the operations of Number itself, in the physical universe, and in the relationship between Number and the physical universe, with which modern science is so familiar, and upon which it depends. In Philolaus' philosophy this logical form is a symbol of something else, which *shows* *itself* subjectively at another level of intelligence – *harmonia*.

Number, Nature, Intelligence and Music

Physical science grounds itself on Number, or mathematical laws, - the 'laws of nature'. Mathematics is now the adopted 'language' of physical science. The work of the physical scientist makes it look as though there is an abstract mathematical reality behind physical existence, and that it is this "form" that the scientist is discovering.

This can too easily be taken to be the divine or semi-divine thing that Pythagoras intuited - Number. Some might even argue that this abstract mathematical matrix is what we should call Reality, parts of which are represented by the physical world. Only parts, though, because there are always exotic areas of pure mathematics that have not yet found an application in physical science, although there seems to be a constant and quite rapid 'movement' from new techniques in pure mathematics to their practical application.

It is the intelligence of the scientist or mathematician who beholds or finds this "form", just as it is intelligence, coupled with the senses, that beholds and scientifically questions the physical world.

Philolaus spoke of 'Nature itself' as being behind the appearance of physical existence. Existence itself, that is, the manifest universe of all existing things, is what Philolaus calls 'Nature in the universe'.[130]

'Nature itself', he said, requires 'Divine intelligence and not human intelligence'.[131] He is not merely saying that God created the universe. What he is saying, in effect, is that Divine intelligence creates nature, and that nature is the reality behind the universe of all existing things. We could go further. We could say that the existential universe is not nature, but merely the manifestation of nature in our less-than-Divine intelligence.

The abstract mathematical "form", which seems to determine what we call the laws of Nature is not Philolaus' 'Nature itself', *because it is grasped by human intelligence*. Number is merely the "substance" of the natural laws that hold together the manifest structure of existence, as determined by *harmonia*. Number is not Nature. Although Number is necessary for existence and for existence to be intelligible, existence comes from the *Being* which is eternal.[132]

Philolaus actually purported to know about *Nature itself.* So he implies that if Nature itself is to be apprehended, then the intelligence of the beholder, in this case Philolaus himself, must itself have changed, to enter the level of the Divine. Here, we are beyond *information*, we are back to an untheoretical metaphysics, to *gnosis*, and the mystical context of *harmonia*.

The transformation of the intelligence of the beholder through subjective knowledge, or through gnosis, was once a deliberate part of the 'alchemical' and Paracelsian study of matter. The scientific study of matter does not have this immediate, conscious aim. In this, finally, is the difference between science and what can properly be called metaphysics.

Both are concerned with knowledge. Science may even be concerned with improving subjective knowledge. But only metaphysics attempts attainment through subjective knowledge, rather than through the study, and gathering of 'objective' information about the world occupied.

We are talking about the belief that what humanity discovers about the world we occupy is already within us, so that understanding the world occupied requires subjective knowledge as well as external observation.

Alchemy and Paracelsianism were attempted methods of initiating this kind of knowledge of the world occupied, together with subjective change, even by 'studying' the world occupied.[133] The study of the nature of the world occupied through Number alone, the purely rational approach, is quite a different thing.

According to Iamblichus and others, Pythagoras helped to bring about subjective change in his disciples through *music*, and the essence of this idea is also central to the Orphic tradition. This was not through the study of music as a science, something that we are told the Pythagoreans also did, but simply through the experience of music.

Similarly, Pythagoras himself is supposed to have received some kind of higher knowledge by 'hearing' the music of the spheres. Again, this was not through scientific, astronomical study. Why could his disciples not hear it? The explanations offered are pseudo-scientific, and assume that this 'hearing' was physical, acoustical.

The singing of the universe need not be acoustical, in the sense that it need not be a phenomena that was part of the world occupied. If it was, then the world Pythagoras occupied was a different world to the one we occupy, and different to the world occupied by his disciples.

The 'objective' aspect of harmony is the acoustical phenomena and form, that which we can measure and understand theoretically as harmony, whereas the subjective side is what we *perceive* as harmony. In Platonism and neo-Platonism harmony has a physical side, and a metaphysical side.

The metaphysical side occurs where 'the soul' is said to be arithmetically 'proportioned', and is therefore in 'correspondence' with arithmetical proportion in the physical world. The implication is that 'the soul' is divided, that is, it is in a condition of conflict that is only stabilised by *harmonia*. Actual, audible, acoustical music can be an aid to this stabilisation. In a sense, music 'tunes the soul'.

But how does it happen? There must be a way in which 'the soul' is ordered or harmonised by the experience of music. Plato portrayed the soul's dividedness quite simply, saying it was in three parts, and that the parts needed to be harmonised rather like the three fundamental musical intervals.

Ptolemy added further subdivisions, giving fourteen species of virtue corresponding to species of musical interval.[134] These 'virtues' are things like moderation, fearlessness and prudence, which are clearly to be encouraged in the subject, i.e. in the soul, and which contribute to the metaphysical harmony, within. The implication in the metaphysical or qualitative harmony of the spheres tradition, as in Orphism, is that music can help to bring about this inner harmony, or virtue.

The crude, quasi-scientific interpretation trotted out in so many accounts, is that the soul, being (or needing to be) arithmetically proportioned in literally the same way as physical or acoustical harmony, just 'responds', and appropriately orders itself or its parts when it hears the right music. But really this is no explanation at all, it is not clearly a metaphor, and it accepts that the 'soul', a metaphysical thing, is literally arithmetically proportioned, precisely like a physical thing.

Literal, arithmetical proportion, must be predicated to something quantitatively measurable, which the soul is not. This kind of 'explanation' is naive, and its attribution to a pre-Socratic teaching, is merely retrospective.

The metaphysical soul cannot literally resonate like a physical body, or be brought into tune by exposure to acoustical vibration. The idea that it can, arises from conceiving the soul as an object, rather than as the reality of the subject.

It is the subject who feels the benefits of music, and who seems to be affected by music. It is the subject who is affected by the object of music, or by his or her subjective experience of the objective, acoustical phenomena. What is missing from this quasi-scientific explanation is an account of how the subjective effect or experience is connected to the objective, acoustical phenomena.

Only the more qualitative accounts like those of Iamblichus, are less naive, and treat the whole question more metaphysically, perhaps in terms of the soul's allegiance to divine harmony, from whence it came, and of which earthly music is a reminder.[135]

The Metaphysical *Harmonia Mundi*

Pythagoras is supposed to have been the first to use the word Cosmos, a word which signifies both order and beauty.[136] The double significance of the word reflects the two aspects of Pythagoreanism, the quantitative and the qualitative. I have suggested that the quantitative side provides useful material for our understanding of the emergence of science. For example, Pythagoras is perhaps most famous for his right-angled triangle theorem which is an important foundation stone of mathematics, science and engineering.

I have also suggested that this useful 'emergence of science' material had a concomitant, qualitative and metaphysical face at the time of Pythagoras. However, from a philosophical point of view, the usefulness of the 'historicity of ideas' filter on the qualitative face, is severely limited for the reasons I have outlined. I have described the quantitative tradition of *harmonia mundi* as a large but spurious plume of smoke, that smoke-screens the truth behind the origins of the metaphysical, *harmonia mundi* idea.

From what fire does this smoke arise? It is a fire started by making quantitative interpretations of the qualitative or metaphysical, and it was encouraged to start because one of the modes of expression of metaphysical ideas, was Number, or quantification.

It was also catalysed by the simultaneous knowledge and use of Number as an actual quantitative tool, and by the fact that 'Number' includes 'proportion' in the wider context of geometry, which can express relationships indescribable by whole number ratios (irrational numbers).

The creation of this quantitative smoke is not something for which only modern interpreters are responsible. Pythagoras' closest disciple may well have created it too, as far as we know. The qualitative or metaphysical, and the quantitative or 'scientific' are both present in the world, then and now. Both were expressed by the ancient sources collectively, often side by side in the same source, and both would probably have been expressed by Pythagoras.

We now turn to the qualitative side of *harmonia mundi*. The metaphysical side of the *harmonia mundi* tradition reports on how Pythagoras, who was himself 'fashioned by the Divine spirit', 'heard' the harmony of the spheres and endeavoured to communicate to those he taught, something of what the divine music communicated to him. [137]

He also is supposed to have carried out somatic and spiritual healing with the use of music, and to have educated his pupils, and ordered their emotions by playing the lyre. [138] The closeness of these reports to the mythical Orphic tradition is notable.

These reports are from much later sources, in particular, Iamblichus. The fragments of Archytas, as we have seen, throw no significant light upon the metaphysical, mystical, or qualitative side of Pythagoreanism. The cosmology of Philolaus, on the other hand, raises some rather interesting questions in this respect.

Before turning to Philolaus, it must first be noted that the authenticity of the fragments attributed to him have long been disputed. [139] However, Freeman indicates this is

50

without justification,[140] and Huffman states that the core of the fragments are now accepted as authentic.[141] We will here treat the contents of the fragments themselves on an equal footing with the attestations by Aëtius and Achilles.

Thanks to Aristotle, Philolaus is much quoted for allegedly having said that everything is Number. But what he said was: 'Actually, everything that can be known has a Number; for it is impossible to grasp anything with the mind or to recognise it without this'.[142] Some have deduced from this that Number was for Philolaus and the Pythagoreans the fundamental 'stuff of the universe', or in some way the 'essence' of the universe.

This is an over-simplification. Number may be a pre-requisite of an existence that is intelligible to the human mind, for this existence consists of a multiplicity of things, and is hence, governed by Number. Number is thus an ordering principle governing the physical 'stuff' of the universe, which according to Philolaus is Earth, Water, Air, and Fire,[143] but Number is obviously not itself the physical 'stuff' of the universe. Is it the ultimate metaphysical or abstract 'essence' behind the physical stuff? Not at all.

Philolaus talks at length about Number, ascribing to it all kinds of metaphysical significance. He even states that the Decad (ten-ness) is the 'origin of divine and human life...'.[144] Nevertheless, Number or the Decad is not the highest point of Philolaus' cosmogony.

He also speaks of The One, the eternal Being of things, Nature, the Non-limited, the Limiting, and *Harmonia*, - none of which are actually subordinated to Number. He makes it clear that there are 'supernatural and divine existences'[145] in which the power of Number operates, without suggesting that these 'supernatural and divine existences' are synonymous with The One, Being, or even Nature.

Most important is Philolaus' statements that Number is 'the cause of recognition',[146] and that it is 'impossible to grasp anything with the mind or to recognise it',[147] without Number. However, he also states it would be 'impossible for any existing thing to even be recognised by us', without the eternal 'Being of things'.[148] Does this perhaps mean that Number is the eternal 'Being of things', the highest principle behind everything? I think not, for the following reason.

Divine intelligence is not human intelligence, for Philolaus says 'Nature itself requires divine and not human intelligence'.[149] Yet when Philolaus says 'it is impossible to grasp anything with the mind or to recognise it'[150] without Number, the mind he refers to is surely the human mind. He is asserting that Number is pre-requisite to existence as it is perceived and understood by the human mind. He says that no things in existence 'would be clear to anyone either in themselves or in their relationship to one another unless there existed Number and it essence'.[151]

If there is such a difference between divine and human intelligence as Philolaus suggests, then we might suspect Number is necessary for human intelligence, but not for the divine. It is impossible for human intelligence to grasp anything without Number, but it is also impossible for human intelligence to grasp Nature itself. That requires divine intelligence.

Number seems to be no help to the human mind in knowing Nature itself. Might it not be that Nature itself does not require Number, and only requires Number when it is 'fitted into' physical existence, and becomes 'Nature in the universe'? Philolaus is quite clear that there is a difference between 'Nature in the universe' and 'Nature itself'. What we have here, again, is the notion of the physical representation or symbolism of something metaphysical. 'Nature in the universe' is the physical symbol of a transcendental, metaphysical 'Nature itself'. If this is the case, then Number also, as known by human intelligence, can be no more than a symbol of 'Nature itself'.

The inference is that the intelligence of the human species, the existence of the human species as sentient beings in a physical existence, and Number or plurality, are all interconnected. Physical existence literally 'makes sense' to human intelligence, through Number.

The corollary to this interpretation is found where Philolaus says 'Number, fitting all things into the soul through sense-perception, makes them recognisable and comparable with one another....',[152] and perhaps even more so where he says of existing things that 'Number gives them body...'.[153]

As Iamblichus later said, 'Number is the ruling and self-created bond which maintains the everlasting stability of the contents of the universe'.[154] True enough. But we cannot assume that Number is The One, or Nature itself, or 'higher' or more important than either of them.

As I have already indicated, although Nature itself requires divine intelligence, it is nonetheless 'fitted together' in the universe from the Non-limited and the Limiting, which make up existing things.[155] This, I am suggesting, is a transition from the metaphysical One, to the physical and the many, through Number, and through Harmonia. It is not clear from Philolaus whether *Harmonia* is a part of Nature or if it is Nature, or another principle.

What is the basic Being of things, if it is not Number, and where does it come from? Philolaus states that 'The One is the beginning of everything' and that 'The first composite...the One, which is in the centre of the sphere, is called Hearth'.[156] We are also told that 'The universe is one, and it began to come into being from the centre....'[157] These statements collectively conjoin the physical universe with the metaphysical One.

Continuing our line of interpretation, the physical universe as it appears through Number, is really the metaphysical One, or the original Being, appearing in physical form, in plurality, intelligible to sense-perception, or sense-perception based intelligence.[158] Is this not basically the same kind of scenario found in the ancient Indian Vedas, dating from approximately the same era?

Should we not also mention once again the three cosmic steps of Vishnu, for we have here firstly The One, with which we may associate divine intelligence and Nature, secondly 'supernatural and divine existences' with which Philolaus still associates Number, and thirdly earthly existence and 'human activities'[159] in the physical universe, also governed by Number?

Philolaus may have sung the praises of Number as a quantitative tool, he may even have indulged in numerology, and made what appear to be 'scientific' speculations, but Number in his philosophy was undoubtedly metaphysically significant. Philolaus' passage on Harmony[160] is quantitative, but Harmony is something that also plays a fully mystical and metaphysical role in the discourse, at the same time as being expressed quantitatively through Number.

In Philolaus' cosmogony, it is said, the whole universe came into existence through measures, weights, numbers, geometry, arithmetic and music,[161] and in his cosmology he asserts that the Earth is not at the centre of the cosmos, but moves in a circular orbit like the other planets, around the mysterious fiery centre called the 'House of Zeus', 'Hearth of the World', 'Altar', 'Meeting-place', or 'Goal of nature'.[162] This 'Hearth' was the 'first thing harmonised'.[163]

The Hearth is synonymous with The One, the beginning of everything.[164] In *De Caelo*, Simplicus tells us Philolaus maintained that the periphery of the universe was another fire 'at the highest point'. The centre was said to be 'first in rank', and around it move in a choral dance ten divine bodies: the sphere of fixed stars, the five planets, sun, moon, earth, and counter-earth.[165] A fragment by Claudianus Mamertus indicates that Philolaus is supposed to have written in a volume entitled 'On rhythms and measures' that the soul is joined to the body through number and harmony, and that Harmony is incorporeal. [166]

Here we have a constant admixture of the metaphysical and the physical, of the qualitative and quantitative. The 'emergence of science' interpretation typically yields a cosmology with a 'fire' at the centre of the celestial system, around which orbits the planets, sun, moon, earth and stars. Around the entire periphery would be the 'fire at the highest point of the universe'.

This in the past was the usual interpretation of Philolaus' cosmology. But why is the Hearth at the centre called by its other names? What is the significance of these? Are these not metaphysical or mystical implications? Even if they are derived from previous 'mythology', what is their significance if not metaphysical? It is true that the oldest

Greek mythology equates the celestial bodies with Gods, or 'living Beings', but what are such assertions if not metaphysical?

As it is reported, there were three 'fires' or suns in the Pythagorean universe as taught by Philolaus. This seems to be the earliest extant source for the many concepts and representations of a 'threefold sun' that subsequently appear in esoteric and 'mystical' literature. We have already seen the weakness of the argument that celestial entities were invented purely for numerological reasons. The three-fold nature of the 'fire' in the universe is commented upon by Aëtius and Achilles.[167]

Heath's translation of Aëtius is:

> 'Philolaus the Pythagorean holds that the sun is
> transparent like glass, and that it receives the reflection
> of the fire in the universe and transmits to us both light
> and warmth, so that there are in some sort two suns,
> the fiery in the heaven and the fiery from which it is
> mirrored, as it were, not to speak of a third also, namely
> the beams which are scattered in our direction from the
> mirror by way of reflection [or refraction]; for we give
> this third also the name of sun, which is thus, as it were,
> an image of an image'.[168]

Heath's translation of Achilles' report is:

> 'Philolaus says that the sun receives its fiery and radiant
> nature from above, from the aetherial fire, and
> transmits the beams to us through certain pores, so

that according to him the sun is triple, one sun being
the aetherial fire, the second that which is transmitted
from it to the glassy thing under it which is called the
sun, and the third that which is transmitted from the
sun in this sense to us.'[169]

Do these not sound like second-hand reports of something that had been heard or read by the attestors, but not really understood? There are certainly a number of things about these attestations that suggest an inadequacy in the frequently encountered, standard 'scientific' interpretation, which portrays a peripheral 'fire', an orbiting sun, and a central fiery 'Hearth', all as parts of a physical, celestial system.

The attestations state that there are 'three suns' or that 'the sun' is 'threefold'. The first kind of 'sun' is an 'aetherial fire' in the 'cosmos' or 'universe'. This is the 'fiery in the heaven'. There is no intrinsic reason why this need be interpreted primarily as a physical, rather than a metaphysical 'fire', but any quasi- or proto-scientific interpretation may of course treat it as physical, as the 'emergence of science' interpretation inevitably will.

The second kind of sun is 'transparent like glass', and it 'reflects' or mirrors the original sun, yet we are also told that it mysteriously 'strains' the heat and light through to us, 'through certain pores'. What does this mean?

And what of third kind of sun?

The third sun, if we are to read the attestations as an early 'scientific theory', can only be a virtual optical image. In other words, ignoring the mysterious 'straining' and the equally mysterious 'through certain pores', we can say the true aetherial, surrounding sun, is 'reflected' by the glassy object, and what we see, is the reflection. But this would not be an 'image of an image', would it?

We would not call this reflection an 'image of an image' unless we are specifically talking about the optical 'real image' on the retina of the eye, and we considered the reflection at the 'glassy object' as an optical 'real image' (which no such reflection is). Are we really, in any case, dealing with this degree of sophistication of optical science? Aëtius thought that this third sun was 'the beams' which are reflected off the 'glassy' sun and 'scattered in our direction'.

This seems to indicate he accepted the virtual image in the glassy object as the third sun, and the aetherial fire and glassy object itself as the first 'two suns'. But he is confusing about this because he says the second sun is 'from' or 'mirrored from' the first. This would not be true of the 'glassy object' itself. How does the glassy reflector itself 'come from', or how can it be 'mirrored from' the true aetherial fire?

We are saying that the aetherial fire is the first sun, the 'glassy thing' itself is the second, and the reflection of the aetherial fire, in the 'glassy thing', is the third sun. The first two of these are real objects, and the last is a virtual image or reflection. In this scenario, how is it that this last sun can possibly be an 'image of an image'? Of course, it is not an 'image of an image' at all. It is just an image.

Achilles is perhaps more consistent with the 'scientific theory' interpretation because he at least seems to call the second and third 'suns' the actual beams which are transmitted or sent in two stages from the aetherial fire.

The trouble here is that we would have four 'suns' including the glassy object itself.

The fact of the matter is that the translations do not make sense. I am not suggesting that that there is anything philologically wrong or inaccurate about the translations. I am suggesting that perhaps Achilles and Aëtius did not themselves understand what Philolaus had taught, or that the translations have fallen foul of a 'scientific theory' hermeneutical approach that is misplaced, - or possibly both.

If Achilles and Aëtius did not understand Philolaus, that could be either because they failed to grasp Philolaus' scientific theory, if indeed that is what it was, or much more likely because they were trying to understand as a quasi-scientific or physical system, something that had once been a wholly metaphysical, mystical, or mythical account. The tendency to interpret a discourse only as a physical theory is not exclusively ours.

Aëtius also concluded in the most pragmatic and quasi-scientific way that Empidocles thought of the sun as a 'reflection of the fire about the earth'.[170] Empidocles' poem *On Nature* does include apparently physical astronomical descriptions but the context of the poem is deeply metaphysical, its details often mythical or mystical, and its use of poetic allegory unmistakable. In *Katharmoi* (Purifications) Empidocles even declares that he himself is a 'god' who has overcome mortality.[171]

The fact is that a 'scientific theory' interpretation of Philolaus' threefold sun, whether ancient or modern, is incomplete and unsatisfactory, quite apart from the unresolved problem of the 'pores' and the 'straining through'. The notion of a 'reflection of a reflection' or an 'image of an image' has about it a fascinating ring, and it is something that could easily endure many generations of repetition, without being understood in its original context.

A metaphysical vision may be uttered, but when it falls upon quantitative ears, the result is always conflict and senselessness, like the idea of the visible sun as a physical 'image of an image'. How many times does this kind of misunderstanding occur in the Greek sources themselves?

Is it not this problem of interpreting metaphysical allegory literally, that undermined Empidocles' sincere statement that the sun 'flashes back to Olympus with serene countenance',[172] a statement that Plutarch reported was a laughing matter?[173]

Whatever physical celestial system Philolaus may have been describing, the notion that the visible sun is an 'image of an image', if taken metaphysically in the context I have indicated, simply means that the visible sun is two stages removed from its metaphysical Sire. In the metaphysical context I have outlined, each 'reality' or 'world' is merely an 'image' - pertinent to the intelligence associated with that 'reality' or 'world' - of a higher 'reality' or 'world' that itself requires some 'higher intelligence'.

This is precisely the kind of interpretation that neo-Platonism would, and does make. In this way, the real sun is filtered through to human perception through the 'levels of mind' or intelligence, and each sun can be said to have 'come from' or to have 'sprung from' (ἀπὸ) its higher source. There is indeed now a sense in which 'sun' is 'sent from' the higher representation or source, and 'towards' the lower representation (πεμπόμενον & πρὸς).[174]

The situation could be described as follows: The 'aetherial fire' or 'fire in the universe' is a metaphysical 'fire'. This may well have been allegorically described like a physical fire, whose symbolic position is surrounding creation. It may even have been thought to be physically present in some way, but if so, its physical presence would nonetheless have been seen as only symbolically significant or important.

Beneath the aetherial fire ('beneath' in the metaphysical, rather than spatial sense) is its symbol or image, the Hearth at the centre. However, the Hearth, like an earthly fire-hearth, is not in itself fiery. It is metaphysically present as the origin of the celestial system, and an intermediary between the metaphysical 'aetherial fire', and what we perceive sentiently as light and warmth.

Its status, by very crude analogy, is not unlike the black-body that the sun is considered to be in physics, when regarded as a perfect black-body radiator, except that in this case it is a kind of metaphysical window or filter, rather than a black body. The light and warmth that we see is not the real sun at all, but its appearance in sense, or in the intelligence of sentient beings - in human intelligence, rather than divine intelligence.

However, there is a further complication. The visible 'sun' is identified with the Hearth, which itself is metaphysically 'the centre' of the system, - and yet at the same time the visible 'sun' is observed in its appearance to move around the Earth. Both the visible 'sun' and the Earth are in later sources said to 'dance around the centre'. In this sense the visible sun cannot be at the physical centre of the system, where the Hearth is supposed to be.

Now if the spatial positioning of the bodies is mystically symbolic, then the actual or speculated physical bodies in space and time are of secondary importance to what they signify. Thus, in terms of the mystical symbolism, the visible sun is not only describable as a reflection or image of the Hearth, but it could also be validly said that it *is* the Hearth (as it is perceived in human intelligence).

In other words the Hearth itself is not directly perceivable in human intelligence, but it is perceived as the moving visible sun. In much the same way, it can be said that the entire universe, though appearing as a multiplicity, is The One, and yet at the same time it is not, for it is multiplicity. Apparent contradiction or paradox is not unusual in mysticism. On the contrary, this is one of its most obvious characteristics.

Similarly, there is a logical conflict between heliocentricity and geocentricity when each is considered in physical terms, but when the meaning of each is metaphysical. Both states of affairs can in a sense co-exist simultaneously. In a metaphysical context this relativity of understanding is neither difficult to conceive, nor something only rarely found.

McEnvoy has recognised an aspect of this, calling it 'valuational heliocentrism', meaning that the sun was understood to occupy a central position in every sense except the physical.[175] The inference is that the celestial system of Pythagoras, even though described in physical terms, is in effect a metaphysical paradigm and not a scientific paradigm.

Thus, if the final image of the originating One in the physical universe is the visible sun, then the 'image of an image' description indicates a three-fold metaphysical 'descent' from The One, to the visible sun. What we see as the sun is not the real sun at all, but the symbol or image of the real sun in physical existence.

The real sun is not a 'thing' as we would know a 'thing', - it is *being* at a metaphysical level, in the eternal act of creation, a stage in the descent of intelligence from The One, to earth and sense-bound human intelligence, where it appears as the visible sun. Even the Sire of the visible sun, called the Hearth at the centre, or later called the glassy object, requiring a higher intelligence to apperceive, is not the originating One itself, but a representation of the One.

A similar three-fold descent, or ascent if you like, is found in Dionysian cosmology, where it appears as the three realms, the terrestrial, the celestial, and the supercelestial. The role of the sun in this context was, for example, recognised by Fludd's brilliant student Pico della Mirandola,[176] who says in *Heptaplus* that fire appears in three ways.

There is the physical element, there is the fire in the sky (the Sun), and there is the metaphysical above existence as the super-celestial seraphic intellect. But they differ, he says, in that the elemental fire burns, that celestial fire enlivens, and the super-celestial loves.[177] Here, he indicates a super-celestial reality above existence.

So here are Philolaus' three suns, described in the neo-Platonic, metaphysical context. The lowest sun is the physical, visible sun, and above it are two higher, metaphysical fires, the highest of which is love. We should not be at all surprised to find ourselves confronted primarily with the metaphysical significance of the sun in Pythagorean cosmology.

The correlation between the visible sun and the Divine is something that is frequently encountered across the whole gamut of times and cultures. It is only quasi-scientific opinion or the hermeneutic filters I have mentioned, that choose to explain the correlation on materialistic grounds alone.

The common idea that the association of the sun with the Divine, originates as a cultural belief arising from our obvious physical dependence upon the sun, is shallow and naive. In Plato's Republic the sun is treated as the image of the good,[178] in a metaphysical context that cannot simply be dismissed or explained in this way.

The presence of the ideas of light, heat, and fire, as metaphysical images related to both the good, and to purgatory, are ubiquitously encountered in theological thought. Zeno the Stoic is reported by Augustine to have thought that God Himself was fire, and reported by Stobaeus to have said that the celestial bodies, endowed with mind and wisdom, were made of creative fire.[179]

The role of fire and light both within Christianity and also in vigorous contention with it, is very much in evidence in the middle ages.[180] In Christian Hermeticism there could even be an identification of Christ with the sun.[181] The attributes of the sun can equally be metaphors of the good and of purgatory, representing as it does, benevolent light and warmth, and at the same time, burning heat and blinding light that cannot be directly faced.

These metaphors occur frequently in patristic discourses that are deeply metaphysical or mystical, and are widely respected as having a content that cannot be dismissed as mere reiterations of mythic or cultural tradition, even though they may employ traditional images.[182]

The metaphor of light, and the idea of a descent from the metaphysical into the physical, i.e. from the One into matter, was highly developed by the neo-Platonists, by whom the number of stages seen in the descent was increased.[183]

Soul, sun, and elemental fire were all active causes for Marsilio Ficino,[184] who wrote a treatise on both corporeal and incorporeal light, in which he discussed their relationship. He declared that the Sun can signify God Himself to the highest degree, and that God's eternal power and divinity can be apprehended through the Sun.[185]

In England the light metaphor was propounded by the Elizabethan magus John Dee, who in his *Propaedeumata Aphoristica* treated light as the first and most sublime creation, and circular motion as perfect. Although Dee assumed the geocentric celestial system of Ptolemy, it was the sun that was given the central symbolic status in both his *Propaedeumata Aphoristica* and the *Monas Hieroglyphica*.[186]

Johannes Kepler is today is a major figure in the 'emergence of science' way of understanding the past, as he was the discoverer of the three laws of elliptical planetary motion that put an end to the ancient ideal of circular orbits. But despite Kepler's 'scientific successes', he was immersed, like Newton and many other figures who are important in the 'emergence of science', in metaphysical thought, and he saw the celestial system in terms of its metaphysical and symbolic significance.

Like the ancient Greeks, he dealt both in metaphysics and in the quantitative science that later divorced itself from its metaphysical companion. His metaphysical view of the celestial system, again, recognises the symbolic status of the sun, being at the centre, at rest, and the cause of motion. Motion of course occurs in Plato and in the Hermetica as associated with time itself, the unreal 'world of becoming'.[187]

In the Hermetica (now thought to be largely derived from Plato) motion is associated with suffering. In Platonic terms, the world of motion, coming to be, and ceasing to be, is an unreal copy of the Real, The One, or God, which is eternally Being, but never becoming or ceasing to be. Kepler sees all this symbolised by the celestial system. He sees the sun as at rest and as the source of motion, and as the image of God the Father and Creator.[188]

The full metaphysical significance of not only the sun, but the whole celestial system, cannot be touched upon by the 'emergence of science' interpretations, or even by the of 'history of myths and ideas' interpretations that pervade scholarship of the Greek sources, especially where they are coloured by a preference for quantitative or physical explanations.

The preference for quantitative and physical understanding, whether that preference is shown by an ancient Greek, or by a space-age scholar, cannot acknowledge the metaphysical significance of 'aetherial fire' (with which the sun is of course associated), and will inevitably take an idea like 'fire above' to mean physically above, rather than above in the metaphysical sense.

Similarly, 'fire in the earth' will be taken to be derived from a physical source like volcanic activity, rather than seeing volcanic activity as a living metaphor for something metaphysical, in relation to Man's mystical experience. In the mystical view, the entire physical universe is a metaphor.[189]

The traditional associations between fire, purgatory or hell, the 'black' or 'invisible' sun, and even the 'fire in the Earth' of the alchemical tradition,[190] are as much a metaphysical interpretation of the human condition, and the spiritual endeavour to overcome it, as they are about the physical structure of the Earth and solar system.

Alchemical transmutation in this context is not merely about gold-production, but about the metaphysical transformation of the alchemist, the transmutation of the human spirit through gnosis.[191] Even if it is true that an imaginative metaphysical belief-system can be built upon observations of natural phenomena, any truly mystical understanding of human purgatory and transformation was arguably far more likely to have originated with the subjective experience of purgatory and transformation, or at least the search for it.

In this context, a physical phenomenon like volcanic activity exists, like the universe as a whole, as merely a physical symbol of the inner search. It is the actual inner journey of the seeker-after-truth, that would, so to speak, determine the interpretation of natural phenomena.

Whilst the details of Philolaus' celestial system considered as a metaphysical symbol may remain obscure, the metaphysical interpretation of the Pythagorean Hearth is easy to see when it is acknowledged how much of what is said in the earliest sources is primarily allegorical in nature.

It is very difficult to see through allegory without some foreknowledge of the possible meaning, but when we know what the story is really about, the allegory by which it is being told becomes relatively transparent. The problem with the 'emergence of science' and the 'history of myths' filters is that they can contain no such foreknowledge.

The finer and even the more general points of the metaphysical philosophy are not exactly visible or tangible to science. Also, if it is an intrinsic part of that philosophy, that historicity is mere illusion, then what does the historicity filter have to offer towards seeing through the allegory, and understanding that philosophy?

Heraclitus said 'Harmony consists of opposing tension, like that of the bow or lyre...', but he also said 'The bow is called Life, but its work is Death'. This, again, is poetic allegory. The Greek word for 'Life' is actually punned with the Greek word for 'bow'.[192] The work of the bow and arrow, as we all know, is death.

It is sheer negligence to appreciate the pun, but not to ask what Heraclitus meant by indicating that the *work* of Life is death, *and that both are related to harmony*. We could explain this in any number of rational ways if we really wanted to, but we should find ourselves running fast into confusion if we are too quick to avoid the metaphysical and offer only 'rational' explanations for everything that is said by an ancient Greek Godman-scientist.

What are we to make of his assertion that 'When you have listened, not to me but to the Logos,[193] it is wise to agree that all things are one'?[194] Or what of the statement that 'Time is a child playing a game of draughts; the kingship is in the hands of a child'?[195]

What we have in the source is the poetic allegorical expression of a connection between Time, Life, death, and Harmony, all of which are ingredients of Plato's metaphysics, all are ingredients of the Myth of Er. All are proper and correct ingredients in the metaphysical idea of the harmony of the spheres.

It is these elements that we should consider now, today, as relevant to our understanding of the meaning of music in the most profound sense, for they have nothing legitimate to do with mistaken ideas about the structure of the celestial system, but everything to do with music and the human emotional condition when it is understood in its full context.

It is assumed that Plato must have had an earlier source from which the Myth of Er was derived.[196] The true source of the Myth of Er is *the metaphysical world-view out of which it springs*. Can we understand the Myth of Er without understanding the philosophy from which it springs, a philosophy that challenges the common notion of time and historicity?

We have to see that from the point of view of that metaphysical philosophy itself (a branch of which is *explicitly* represented by Plato), the meaning of the myth is incompatible with the opinion that the myth has its source somewhere in time. Anyone who sticks only to the historical facts and thinks, like so many scholars, that the myth must have its source in time, clearly has no empathy for, or understanding of its philosophical content and meaning.

In Plato's philosophy, the manifest, objective aspect of the world is seen as unreal, and veiling an underlying unity or Reality, identified as The One.[197] This central idea of unity would be very much expected of any philosophy or tradition that was fundamentally mystical.

As Combs has put it, in his tackling the problem of the meeting ground between science and spirit: 'most mystical traditions share the idea that while multiplicity and separateness are characteristics of manifest reality, the

69

deep order is one of mutual enfoldment and oneness'.[198] Only this unified world-view can support the assertion that the 'universe sings'.[199]

The strength and continuity of the
harmonia mundi tradition

The mathematical study of musical intervals, and their combination to form modes and scales, is the basis of musical science as it was widely studied throughout most of the history of Western music. Before the 'scientific revolution' of the seventeenth-century, the science of music was not a mere adjunct to other intellectual pursuits, but rather, its place in the *quadrivium* indicates its status as an essential part of the learned man's studies.

Musical science was important to the understanding of the world, and of Man and his place in the macrocosm. The importance of musical science, or the science of 'harmonics' as it was known, was supported by, and arguably derived from, the impressive strength of the quantitative harmony of the spheres tradition.

The idea of the harmony of the spheres has always had its opponents in one way or another, the first obvious example being Aristotle. Nevertheless, the celestial system that was accepted in Europe for fifteen centuries until the scientific revolution, was the system originated by Ptolemy, who was an important proponent of cosmic harmony.

Ptolemy developed many ideas inherited from Plato, concerning both the quantitative and metaphysical faces of *harmonia mundi*. He could indeed be recognised by modern acousticians as a representative of the quantitative tradition, and even as what one scholar has described as a 'number cruncher',[200] but at the same time he clearly accepted Plato's conception of the arithmetically proportioned soul, and that the effects of music were due to the kinship between the 'harmonics' of the soul, and the harmonic structure of musical phenomena.[201]

Ptolemy developed an extensive astrological correlation between the heavens, music, and the human soul.[202] 'Harmonics' was for Ptolemy, not merely a quantitative science, but a manifestation of a predictable, divinely ordained order.[203]

Knowledge of this 'divine' order is both subjective and theoretical and it is a function of nature that allows subjective perception of the divine order.[204] Ptolemy saw the 'power of attunement' as present everywhere, but as revealed most in human souls and the celestial motions. He declared the power of harmonia to be the Platonic form that causes reason.[205]

St Augustine, Pseudo-Dionysius and Boethius were important in transmitting Platonism and neo-Platonism to the middle ages.[206] Boethius was instrumental in propagating the musico-mathematical concepts from Plato's *Timaeus* and ensuring that musical science occupied an important position in scholarship.[207]

He also made references to Philolaus' music theory and quoted definitions of musical intervals that he attributed to Philolaus.[208] His treatises *De institutione musica*, *De institutione arithmetica*, and the influential *Consolations of Philosophy* all present music and mathematics as necessary to the attainment of knowledge and virtue,[209] and in *De institutione musica* he emphasises hearing for its ability to influence the soul.[210]

Boethius helped establish music as one of the disciplines of the *quadrivium* together with arithmetic, geometry, and astronomy,[211] and so to make it essential to what was considered a complete understanding of the world. Boethius' interpretation of Plato, and the theses he developed from him, emphasise 'reason' as an authority.

Boethius seems to understand 'reason' as an intellectual, or even deductive faculty, that can be enhanced through intellectual study. In this he sides mostly with the spirit of the quantitative tradition, and the common belief that the teaching of Pythagoras was a celebration of Man's true authority, an authority that is a kind of abstract or God-given 'reasoning' power, over sense,[212] a 'reasoning' power that is in general not distinguished from the intellectual faculty that is employed in the study of arithmetic or geometry.

Boethius endorsed a metaphysical correspondence, at least theologically, between the various manifestations of *musica* with which his name is associated, but musical scholarship in the Boethian sense was primarily a scientific or quasi-scientific study.

Later scholars continued to expand of the study of music as a science,[213] and two thousand years after Plato, in renaissance cosmology, the notion that musical principles permeate the cosmos at every level, once again reached grand proportions.

There now existed a strong movement of philosophers who used harmonic models of the cosmos and also pursued the study of practical music, but whose motives were distinct from orthodox musical scholarship.[214]

They not only studied the quantitative complexities of harmonic science, but also sought a qualitative, deeper metaphysical understanding of music as an affective power. In this pursuit there seems to have been a good deal of cross-fertilisation of the 'music cosmology' indirectly inherited from the Pythagorean tradition, with the occult, neo-Platonic and Hermetic philosophies.

The latter had spread following the rediscovery of the *Corpus Hermeticum*, which was initially embraced as a source of ancient Egyptian wisdom, perhaps more authoritative than Plato, since it was held to contain esoteric teachings transmitted from the Egyptian god Thoth.[215]

By the height of renaissance, the Elizabethan magus and Hermeticist John Dee was treating music as a mystical art capable of putting Man in tune with the universal order,[216] and in Jacobean England the metaphysical structure of the cosmos was documented in vivid detail by Robert Fludd, who disclosed the secrets of his music-cosmology in his monumental but unfinished *History of the Macrocosm and Microcosm*.[217]

Fludd's cosmology was built on an already thriving and complex foundation of ideas linking Man with the cosmos as a whole, in a metaphysical and symbolic way. Those ideas included the neo-Platonic concept of the 'Great Chain of Being'[218] in which everything that existed either physically or incorporeally, was linked in a hierarchy descending from God down through metaphysical levels into the material world.

The universe was understood in the context of a macrocosm-microcosm 'correspondence', in which Man (the microcosm), and the universe (the macrocosm), were complementary symbols of each other.[219] The renaissance notions of macrocosm, microcosm, and harmonic relationship, were variants and elaborations on the tradition inherited from the Greeks and transmitted by

Boethius, who had reiterated them in his own musical theory.[220]

For magi like Robert Fludd or John Dee, the musico-cosmological world-view was part of a matrix of esoteric, mystical knowledge, but the notions of the Great Chain of Being and the macrocosm-microcosm correspondence were themselves expressed more broadly in a variety of ways through Elizabethan art and culture.[221]

This world-view was imbued with Platonism and neo-Platonism, drawing particularly on the fifth century Christian neo-Platonists Dionysius the Areopagite,[222] and Plotinus. Music does not feature as prominently in the *Corpus Hermeticum* as it does in the writings of say, Iamblichus, but it was nevertheless given an important role in the Hermetic subculture that existed as an undercurrent to the neo-Platonic beliefs.

Although no formal academy existed in England for the propagation of Hermetic or occult teaching, its influence reached high culture through the close association of the magus and the aristocracy.[223]

Many of the ideas held by the English magi were derived from earlier continental Hermeticists, who, influenced by the legendary Greek accounts of the marvellous effects of music, had developed their own ideas sometimes to fantastic proportions.[224]

Francesco Giorgi had taken the ideas of *musica mundana, humana* and *instrumentalis* that he had obtained from Boethius, and permeated them with cabalism.[225] As in England, it had been held on the continent that the power of music to affect Man comes from the unity of Man and the cosmos, both of which are subject to, and related by, musical proportion.

Again, this idea was not new. It is, as we have seen, implicit in the earliest Greek tradition, it is epitomised in Plato, and it is explicitly enunciated by later philosophers including Ptolemy and Boethius. Music was thus seen by the Hermetic or occult philosopher as a key to knowledge of the higher levels of being in the Great Chain, and as having the power to affect the inner being to such an extent that it could even induce some kind of higher cosmic awareness.

The correspondences that existed between all things, and between material and incorporeal levels of Being, assisted in the spiritual quest for union with God, and could even be called upon in the ritualised attempt to invoke assistance from the higher levels. Pico della Mirandola's teacher Marsilio Ficino, whom Cosimo de Medici had set the task of translating the Corpus Hermeticum, introduced a new hierarchy of correspondences which he developed from that of Plotinus.[226]

Ficino was himself an instrumentalist, giving frequent performances before a large circle of friends.[227] Working with an occult system that invoked power from the correspondences, Ficino aimed to influence people and events through musico-magic.[228] He believed music to be the medicine of the soul,[229] and to be at its most potent when conjoined with words, enabling 'heavenly gifts' and 'celestial things' to be obtained.[230]

The perfect matching of words with musical sound affected the intellect as well as the spirit, thus influencing the entire human being.[231] These ideas were later absorbed by John

Dee, and adopted by Philip Sidney as the basis of his beliefs in the power of measured verse and music.[232]

Poetry was considered by Ficino to have its origins in the divine mind itself, whereas music had its origins in the harmony of the spheres. However the music of the spheres was held by Ficino to be something essentially divine or metaphysical. His understanding of the effects of music was based upon a metaphysical and astrological view of Man and the macrocosm, in which there is correspondence between earthly and divine music, that can raise earthly perception towards the divine.

On hearing certain 'sweet harmonies and rhythms', the soul is 'exhorted and excited to consider the divine music with a more ardent and intimate sense of mind'. In Ficino we find again the neo-Platonic idea of a hierarchical descent of Being from unity (The One) to physical plurality, and the idea that the manifest physical universe is symbolic of a greater, metaphysical whole.[233]

As far as music is concerned, Ficino is arguably the most important philosopher of the renaissance, and more generally speaking, the most important writer of the Florentine awakening.[234] He was for many years the leader of the Florentine Academy, which although perhaps hardly an academy in the proper sense,[235] seems to have disseminated Platonism widely through those who became associated with it.[236]

Ficino was known and read across Europe, and was a major force in the spread of Platonism in sixteenth century thought.[237] When his philosophy did not meet with the approval of his clerical enemies, his influence seems to have been sufficient to avoid the hostile forces that befell his pupil Pico.[238] His *Book of Life* brought immediate accusations of demonic magic and necromancy, but by enlisting the help of friends from three of the most powerful families in Florence, Ficino succeeded in clearing his name, and averting a Papal ban.[239] He wrote the first complete translation into any Western language of the works of Plato, and published in his *Theologia Platonica* a commentary on Plato's *Symposium*.[240]

The ancient idea of the macrocosm-microcosm correspondence, and the neo-Platonic 'Great Chain of Being' are models - particular ways of expressing a relationship between Man and the cosmos as a meaningful whole. The approach is one that sees the part only in the context of the whole. It is fundamentally a metaphysical interpretation of man's existence and relation to the cosmos, but one that often expresses itself in explicitly quasi-scientific terms.

Unlike Pythagoreanism as a whole, a cosmology like Fludd's, though full of the use of Number and 'quantification', juxtaposes the mathematical and the metaphysical, and does not even try to grasp the full descriptive and predictive power of mathematics. Rather than seeking the objective fact or the quantitative laws governing the parts, it uses mathematical relations to express, symbolise and corroborate a qualitative, subjective view of the workings of the whole.

It contrasts strongly to scientific reductionism and materialism which sees quantitative examination of the parts as the key to understanding the whole as a complexus. Conversely we can envisage even the earliest Pythagoreanism as setting out upon a road exploring the laws of Number and how they relate to the physical world, a road which soon becomes detached from the metaphysical path of which it was once a part. The quantitative road soon becomes the sole occupation of enquiry, and a foundation stone of emerging scientific method.

The 'scientific revolution' of the seventeenth century signifies the dissolution of the musico-cosmological world-view, as musico-cosmology gradually becomes cast into the shadow of 'scientific' cosmology. One great cornerstone of developing scientific cosmology came in the form of the Copernican theory of heliocentricity.

Copernicus' theory appeared in the previous century and asserted on empirical and mathematical grounds that the Earth should be considered as revolving around the Sun and not *vice versa*.[241] Such a suggestion, which was contrary to the teachings of the Church, was first cautiously presented in the guise of a merely 'theoretical model' that happened to be useful for assisting astronomers' calculations. But eventually, assisted by the observations of Galileo, the idea gained acceptance as fact, and in the eyes of the progressive scientists, it cast all geocentric cosmology like Fludd's conclusively into the annals of the past.

Fludd, the last great representative of renaissance Hermeticism, died in 1637. In the very same year Descartes published his *Discourse on the method of rightly conducting one's reason and seeking truth in the sciences...*[242]

The Discourse asserted the independence of mind and body as two distinct 'substances',[243] and in doing so provided a schema for an empirical scientific method based upon the principle of 'objective observation'. The mind could know itself through introspection, but it could also be the independent, objective observer and investigator of the material world. It was capable of being the independent, objective, scientific mind.

In effect, Descartes' duality of matter and mind, succeeded for three hundred years or so in legitimising a separation between subjective knowledge and the pursuit of information about physical nature. Having accepted the duality as a basis for scientific understanding of the world, science now faces the task of ridding itself of that duality.

The scientific world-view, as it matured, offered little support for a cosmology that is founded on mystical principles or metaphysical symbolism, but in its earlier stages we can find examples of the two approaches to understanding the universe, coexisting within the protagonists of scientific method.

One of the better known instances of this coexistence, relating to *musica mundana*, can be found in the case of Kepler. Kepler was what we would now call a scientist. Kepler's three laws of planetary motion are still used today, and are named after him - they not only confirm Copernicus' assertion of heliocentricity, but also, by showing that the planets move in ellipses around the sun, they destroy the ancient sanctification of circular motion.

However, this destruction came about not as a direct act of scientific disregard for the echoes of Platonism, and not as a result of purely mathematical analysis, but actually as result of Kepler's attempts to prove that the orbits of the planets were determined by the shapes of the five Platonic solids.[244] Kepler also continued to study and write on the subject of cosmic harmony[245] and calculated a mathematical basis for the music of the spheres based upon the newly discovered law of non-circular motion.[246]

Even in the late seventeenth century the great Newton himself continued to write abundantly on alchemical and mystical matters. But it is not those writings that determined the course of things to come. In 1687 he published his *Philosophiae Naturalis Principia Mathematica*, which became the revolutionary basis of a new era in cosmology, and laid the foundation of what has become known as classical mechanics.

The remnants of Greek cosmology were finally and firmly overthrown by a handful of relatively simple mathematical formulae that immediately explained a host of known, but puzzling observations. Newton's laws simultaneously explained Kepler's laws, the precession of the equinoxes, minor perturbations in the motions of the planets, and the complex variations in the motion of the moon.[247]

The unequivocal scope of the *Principia* establishes it as a masterpiece, *a tour de force* in the process of disentangling fact from imagination, and more generally, the objective from of the subjective. It is one of the most prominent milestones in the evolution of physics.

What it did, was to blow away centuries of accumulated, spurious quantitative smoke from the harmony of the spheres tradition. Above all, it fired a new intellectual optimism in the combined power of 'objective' empirical observation and mathematical description, an optimism that heralded the ages of reason and enlightenment.[248]

Notwithstanding the new enthusiasm for scientific method, the echoes of macrocosm-microcosm style musico-cosmology continued, not least in the field of medicine. Whilst medicine has always had its share of mechanical philosophers who have chosen to see the human being as a machine, it has also always traditionally posed additional questions with which the physical sciences were not primarily concerned, questions concerning mind and the nature of its connection with the body.

In this context, the use of musical principles in understanding Man's physiological, spiritual and psychological nature existed outside the boundaries of music-cosmology, and persisted in England into the eighteenth century, as Kassler has shown.[249]

In particular, the Baconic view that health is a harmony and that the body is like a musical instrument or consort of instruments,[250] remained a guiding principle in parts of medical practice beyond the seventeenth century.[251]

Twentieth century medicine has witnessed a conceptual rift between body and mind,[252] largely because of an unquestioned, tacit acceptance of a Cartesian-like duality of mind and matter, or mind and body, but also on the strength of its reductionist understanding of the body.

This is now slowly changing in some areas. But in the eighteenth century respected medical writers in England frequently puzzled over the connection of mind and body,[253] and acknowledged the effect of the mind upon the health of the body, and *vice versa*.

The mind-body question provided a medium for the continued speculation on the effects of music upon the human organism, but without the need to endorse the concept of universal or cosmic 'music'. Nevertheless, these physicians were well aware of the Greek and later accounts of the marvellous effects of music, and were fond of quoting them. In addition to the idea that music could affect the vital or animal spirits in the body directly, the mysterious interaction and connection between body and mind, itself allowed a number of English medical writers and practitioners to endorse the medical efficacy of music.[254]

In this respect it was music's power to affect the passions that was held to be important, since the management of the passions was seen as being one of the physician's most valuable tools.[255] The passions were understood to both exasperate and cause diseases, and the mutual influence between mind and body was considered of the greatest importance, especially in cases that we would now call psychosomatic, or cases of depression or anxiety.[256]

The English eighteenth-century acceptance of the medicinal efficacy of music, seems to be associated with the theory of vitalism[257] and on the unanswered question of the connection of mind and body, rather than on some deference to the Wisdom of the ancients. Nonetheless the use of music in eighteenth century medicine noticeably parallels the use of music by Pythagoras', as reported by Iamblichus.[258]

What appears to be repercussions of Platonism or neo-Platonism seems to have thrived in the environs of nineteenth and twentieth century theosophy, and new musical cosmologies have been proposed by Blavatsky, Steiner, Mathers, Jung, Gurdjieff, and Ouspensky.[259]

Composers of the twentieth century have continued to pay tribute the notion of cosmic music,[260] and Jules Combarieu has even equated music with magic, and the composer with the magician, in a quasi-Orphic sense.[261] The echoes continue unabated to the present day.[262]

The Pythagorean Circle
- symbol of *harmonia*

The Pythagorean Circle, or Great Circle of Fifths, is a diagram representing *the harmonia*, or what we would call a scale. The use of diagrams for communicating ideas and as a way of understanding things, implies and invites the use of what might appropriately be called our 'diagrammatical understanding' *modus operandi* of intelligence, that is a part of discursive, conceptual, object-orientated *thinking*.

Object-orientated thinking relates readily to diagrams. Mathematical formulae are in effect abstract *diagrams* of quantity and relationship between quantities. If we can draw a diagram of something, then we understand it in the way that the diagram encapsulates the relationships between symbolised concepts.

Conversely, subject-orientated understanding is not information about concepts and their relationships. It does not arise from concept structures. For example, you cannot draw a diagram of loss of self, or death of self, or absence of self.

Actually, you can, because you can draw a diagram of *anything* you can *conceptualise*, and anything that can be named, including *self*, can be conceptualised. But if you do it will be a diagram of a conceptualisation, which is object-orientated, and it will only relate to object-orientated thinking and the reality *it* creates.

Nevertheless, I am going to present some diagrams to illustrate the connection of harmony, musical scale and universe. Diagrams of a mixed nature, that are supposed to represent something beyond the literal relationship of concepts that appear in them, are found in all kinds of sources especially those primarily concerned with subject-orientated knowledge.

They appear in the form of magical symbols, hieroglyphs, mandalas, cabalistic and arcanic diagrams and symbols, in Hermetic manuscripts, quite frequently as pictures of labyrinths and spirals, and in many other ways.[263] Diagrams that are part of the *music of the spheres* tradition, such as those of Robert Fludd, may in particular include numbers, mathematics, or quasi-mathematics.[264]

Plato's description of the creation of the 'world soul' in *Timeaus* is essentially such a 'mixed' diagram *in textual form*. The diagrams below are less profound in their implications than this. They represents how apparently separate 'elements' that we turn into 'concept centres' in object-orientated thinking, can be interconnected not only because they are part of an overall 'concept-structure', but more importantly because they are part of the *subject-orientated* 'structure' of a whole.

We connect the concepts through *thinking*, but in doing so, we arrive at an object-orientated 'structure' in thought. The diagrams I have used are derived from the Pythagorean Circle. Like the Greek textual 'diagrams', the Pythagorean Circle is not just an object-orientated diagram, because it has a another level of interpretation.

The early Greek *harmonia* is something that 'fits together opposites' and at the same time, or at least in later usage, refers to what we would now call the musical scale, in fact, a tuning or temperament. Roughly speaking, harmony itself, as the whole number ratios that appear in the science of *harmonics*, cannot be used to form the structure of a *harmonia* or scale of twelve intervals to the octave, without introducing disharmony between some notes. This is a consequence of the nature of the Great Circle, and the factual illustration of this is as follows.

Mathematically, harmonic musical intervals are expressed as certain integer ratios.[265] It is said that Pythagoras discovered the harmonic ratios of the 'perfect' intervals and was responsible for calling them 'perfect'. The ratio of the Pythagorean or perfect fifth is 3 : 2 (or 2 : 3) and this can be 'circulated', using a 'Great Circle of Fifths' diagram with modern note names:

Diagram 1:

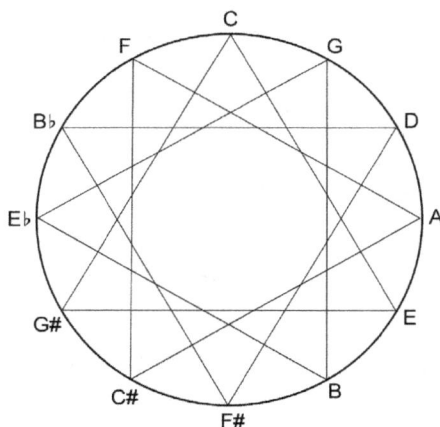

Clockwise progression round the circle represents ascending fifths (or descending fourths), and anticlockwise represents descending fifths (or ascending fourths).[266] The distance progressed in each direction is arbitrary – there is no absolute rule.

Circulation in this particular instance is made clockwise from C round to G# and anticlockwise from C round to Eb. Even in terms of modern musical grammar an 'imperfection' now occurs in the interval from G# to Eb. This is a diminished minor sixth, not a perfect fifth.

We could alternatively have continued from C clockwise right around the circle and back to the top, but we would then finish on B#, not C. Grammatically, the circle does not 'close' – if only one note occupies each position around the circle, then to close the circle it must contain at least one interval that is not a perfect fifth.

The discrepancy is not merely grammatical. Acoustically, the Circle represents the tuning of consecutive fifths (or alternating ascending and descending fourths and fifths within an octave). If eleven fifths are tuned 'perfect', the remaining interval will be smaller than a perfect fifth by an amount known as the comma of Pythagoras.[267]

Similarly, if twelve consecutive ascending perfect fifths are tuned, the final note will not quite be seven perfect octaves above the starting note. It will be sharp from this, again, by the Pythagorean comma.

Mathematically the harmonic ratio of the octave is 2:1 and that of the perfect fifth, 3 : 2. A seven octave interval thus has the harmonic ratio 2^7 and an interval of twelve perfect fifths has the ratio $(3/2)^{12}$. The Pythagorean comma is an interval with the ratio $\{(3/2)^{12}\} : \{2^7\}$.

A scale of twelve intervals to the octave tuned by so-called 'Pythagorean tuning' respects only the perfect fifth (and its inversion the perfect fourth). Twelve fifths contained in the scale can be tuned perfect and the last must by acoustical and mathematical necessity remain a 'wolf'[268] interval, smaller than a perfect fifth by the Pythagorean comma.

Diagram I is the Pythagorean Circle but it also shows straight lines connecting notes defining (clockwise) what we would now call major thirds. Again, grammatically, four of these are 'incorrect' – they are grammatically diminished fourths. Any one of the straight lines subtends clockwise an arc of four fifths (or diminished minor sixths). The arc clockwise from C to E is an interval defined by four perfect fifths.

This simultaneously defines two octaves and a major third C to E. Because the harmonic ratio of a perfect fifth is $3:2$, such an interval has a ratio of $(3:2)^4 = 5.0625$. The harmonic ratio for two octaves is $4:1$, and so the ratio for two octaves and a major third, is $(4:1)\times(5:4) = 5$.

Thus the two octaves and a 'third' defined by the four perfect fifths in the arc of the Circle is an interval greater than two octaves and a harmonic (or 'pure') third. It is wider than two octaves and a harmonic third by the ratio $5.0625:5$, an interval known as the syntonic comma (the comma of Didymus), which is more usually expressed as the harmonic ratio $81:80$.

So, a third defined by perfect fifths is greater than a harmonic third by the syntonic comma. This wide third has subsequently been called the *Pythagorean Third*. Although the syntonic and Pythagorean commas differ, for practical tuning purposes they can be considered the same size.

The other differences may look small, mathematically, but they are substantial, acoustically. The modern musical ear not versed in early music is conditioned to accept all major thirds considerably wider than a harmonic major third, because of the now widely accepted tuning convention called Equal Temperament.

On a modern piano which is tuned this way, all major thirds are the same size, and all are wider than the harmonic third. However, *Pythagorean thirds* would be unacceptably wide even to modern ears, if they were tuned on the piano.

In modern terms, a Pythagorean scale contains three perfectly good, harmonic triads related as I, IV, V, in the major key whose tonic is two semitones below the lowest note of the wolf diminished minor sixth.

However, this I, IV, V relationship of modern major tonality is not likely to have been *musically* significant to Pythagoras, as it is to us. It only arises because the diminished fourths that fall across the 'wolf', which in our diagram is placed between G sharp and E flat, each have practically the same ratio as a harmonic major third.[269]

They are acoustically, for all practical purposes, harmonic major thirds, otherwise known as 'pure' thirds. The other thirds defined by the straight lines are Pythagorean Thirds. There are no attestations that the Pythagoreans ascribed any particular significance to this duality in the 'thirds'. It seems thirds were relatively unimportant to the Pythagoreans.

Thirds, however, became important in time, in musical practice. The size of the wide thirds in a scale can be reduced, and even the unpleasantly narrow 'wolf' can be widened, by deliberately 'tempering' some or all of the 'fifths' so as to 'absorb' some of the adverse effect of the commas.

If, for example, each of the twelve intervals around the circle were to be narrowed by 1/12 of a Pythagorean comma, no 'wolf' interval would appear, and all the thirds would be wider than a harmonic third by only 2/3 of the Pythagorean comma. This is precisely the strategy adopted in the modern convention of Equal Temperament.[270]

I have said *only* 2/3 of a Pythagorean comma, because this is a improvement on the size of the Pythagorean third, which is a whole syntonic comma wider than the harmonic 'pure third'. However, many experienced performers or lovers of early music would declare that this equally tempered third is ugly because it is too wide.

Once one has been initiated into the substantial physical sonority and beauty of true harmonic intervals (which one cannot be whilst confined only to equally tempered musical practice), the significance of all intervals and their intonation shines through to a sensibility now lost to the modern ear conditioned to accept Equal Temperament. To this sensibility there is a place for the piquancy and colour of tempered intervals, but only in relief against the sonority of true harmonic intervals, or intervals that are close to this.

True harmonic intervals are said to be *Justly Intoned*. Just Intonation is a performance possibility for any given interval or vertical harmony, but it is not (as often misunderstood), a method of tuning 'the perfect scale' or a temperament, and no Great Circle or scale of twelve fixed notes can be constructed in which *all* the relations of the notes are Justly Intoned harmonic intervals.

As a performance possibility for music involving free harmonic progression, polyphony or counterpoint, it requires the use of more than one note per position in the scale or Great Circle, or more than one possible pitch per note. The pursuit of Just Intonation using a fixed pitch scale is the reason why Western microtonal scales for practical use are not an invention of the twentieth century as might be supposed, but were of interest even in the sixteenth century.[271]

Now we can address the Circle is a less objective way, to glean its symbolic properties. The Great Circle showing the full complexity and interdependence of all the note pitches and every interval in the twelve note scale is shown in Diagram 2 :

Diagram 2 :

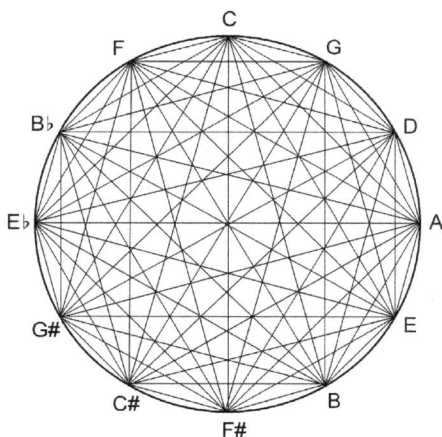

The lines are also lines of *cause and effect* in the *harmonia*, the scale or temperament. No note can be altered without affecting its relationship to every other note, and this affects the *harmonia* or temperament. The diagonals across the circle, are the tritones – the augmented fourths or diminished fifths, the *diabolus in musica* of early theory that was studiously avoided in practice.

In modern music of course, every interval is equally acceptable including that of the *diabolus in musica* which simply becomes another discord that can be prepared and resolved. Nevertheless, in terms of early theory the greatest symbolic disharmony lies in the opposites.

Turning the theory on its head, and looking at the circle in an unconventional way, we can see *it is constructed of disharmonious opposites*, arranged such that the result creates harmony along the other lines of relationship, according to the *harmonia*, the tuning or temperament employed. In keeping with the pre-Socratic notion, *harmonia* creates the harmony by fitting together the disharmonious opposites.

The *whole* circle represents the perfection of the unison or octaves, on which the other relationships depend, and without which the Circle would loose its meaning. The unison, the octave, the multiple octave, and the fifths, before arrangement in the Circle, *are* 'perfect'. But the Circle is not. As a consequence of the mathematics behind the structure it *must* contain the commas – 'imperfection' in the relationships is inherent in the *harmonia*.

Some relationships may be perfect or pure, but it must always be that some will not. Perfect harmony, where it occurs, is the direct result of the *harmonia*, but it is not the *harmonia* itself. The *harmonia* itself, as a means of tempering, applies to the *whole*, and is *necessary* in the first instance because the whole Circle of perfect fifths in actuality cannot ever be the perfect unison or octave that it represents. Starting with C, it circulates not back to C, but to notes of actual, different pitches, B# or D double flat, depending on which way we go.

Why is there discrepancy or imperfection in the mathematical structure behind it all? It would have been very *elegant* of nature if twelve perfect fifths could have exactly equalled seven octaves, and very convenient if four perfect fifths could have exactly equalled two octaves and a harmonic major third.

The inelegance and inconvenience comes from the fact that the scale, or Circle, does *not* occur in nature with Pythagorean, Divinely *perfect* fifths. Harmony, as intervals governed by integer ratios, *is* a part of natural phenomena, but it comes complete with its own "imperfections" and complications that arise when it is manifested in "earthly music".

Mathematically, Western harmony begins with the harmonic number series – 1, 2, 3, 4, 5, 6 etc. The attempt to *arrange* harmony in a *scale* or Circle comes through human beings. The scale itself, if all the notes are heard simultaneously, is arguably a cacophony. In contrast, the harmonic series itself, exhibited in say, the natural behaviour of the monochord, whose tone is made from the harmonic series, is unmistakably heard as both harmony and unison.

The acoustical harmonic series has been called "the chord of nature", and it occurs *everywhere* in nature that there is complex periodic phenomena, though not always acoustically. There is no equivalent 'twelve interval to the octave' "scale of nature" in naturally occurring phenomena.

The cacophony of the scale whose notes are sounded simultaneously is a reminder of the human-made function of the scale. It is not designed (originally) to be sounded simultaneously. It is designed to diffract natural vertical harmony through *time*, to provide a set of acoustical reference points for the activity of extending harmony through time, in what we call music.

When we study acoustical harmony in the scientific, object-orientated way, we deal with it in the context of space and time, and say it is oscillatory phenomena in time. But really, from the musical point of view, any given vertical harmony itself is not in time at all.

Unlike melody, unchanging continuous harmony is not a musical function of time. From the subject-orientated position, pure unchanging continuous harmony does not have an 'objective' time element to it. Any change in it introduces time, not as the clock implies, but as persisting relationship in the awareness, of what was, to what is.

In order to "crystallise" harmony into a set of fixtures, in order to *condition* it so that it can be recreated across *time*, a *harmonia* is necessary, whether deliberately 'worked out' or not. *Harmonia* is a static principle of the whole, that fits everything together, allowing harmony that constantly changes, in time, and necessarily includes disharmony. This much about both senses of the word *harmonia* is clearly present in the symbol of the Pythagorean Circle.

Harmonia, the universe and the soul[272]

It is reported that the Pythagoreans considered the soul to be a kind of *harmonia*, or an 'attunement'. It was said to be 'in' the body as the *harmonia* is 'in' the lyre, when the lyre is in tune. This raised questions concerning other arguments for the immortality of the soul. If a *harmonia* is a consequence of right relationship (proportion) between the strings, then it vanishes when the lyre is destroyed, or the strings go out of tune.

Thus, by analogy the soul must be destroyed when the body, or the condition of right relationship between its vital parts or elements is destroyed, in what is called death. On the other hand, the Pythagoreans are supposed by some of their interpreters to have held there to be a mathematical Reality that is transcendental to the material world.

On this basis, the *harmonia* survives unaffected in mathematical Reality when the lyre is detuned or destroyed, and consideration of the soul as a *harmonia* does not affect its immortality.

In *Phaedo* Socrates argues that the soul is immortal and is not a kind of *harmonia*. The argument rests on the notion that a lyre can be more or less in tune, and contain more or less of a *harmonia*, whereas a soul cannot be more or less of a soul.[273] Also, different souls can possess different qualities of intelligence, goodness, ignorance and wickedness etc., whereas this kind of differentiation and combination of qualities does not exist between *harmonia*s.[274] Clearly the meaning of *harmonia* in the musical context here is that there is but one *harmonia*, one tuning.

This does not mean that Socrates did not relate the concept of *harmonia* to the concept of the soul. He did so but in another way. The idea of *harmonia* occurs in the Myth of Er related by Socrates, but here it is 'transcendental' to the material world, in that it is beyond death - it is not of this world - but rather, it is depicted as the 'harmony' of the great system in which souls are by necessity involved in the cycle of life and death.

However, since it is generally not sensible to take the content of myth literally, and for the reasons I have already argued, we are at liberty to say that in the Myth of Er the transmigration of the soul as a continuing entity from one incarnation to the next, is not a literal 'diagram' of the truth that the myth supposedly stands for.

The actual transmigration of the soul as a continuing entity is not really what reincarnation in the Myth necessarily means. What stands unaltered from Socrates is that there *is* a connection between the idea of *harmonia* and death, and that the difference between a living body and a dead one is that there is *life* 'in' it. What should we say is the relationship between life, death, *harmonia* and 'soul'?

The source of Socrates' wisdom is not discursive thought, but rather, his engagement of it in 'Socratic dialogue' as a means of communication is a "top down" activity of attempting to express self-knowledge in the logical space of thinking. Whether we credit Socrates, Plato, or both for this, matters not – it is the principle that is important.

Unfortunately, Plato is usually interpreted in terms of his 'theories' and 'arguments' and the tenability of the relationships between them. It seems perfectly clear that in Plato 'Reason' as practised by the philosophers, is not merely an intellectual search for knowledge, but includes the practice of self control, self responsibility, the pursuit of self-knowledge, and ultimately is about finding the truth of death.

In the arena of discursive argument Socrates utilises all kinds of ideas and pre-existent beliefs as the medium of communication. When the discussion enters the area of knowledge beyond death, the discursive method in Plato is abandoned, and communication through direct mythical discourse takes over.

In *Phaedo* Socrates' argument that the soul existed previously to its current incarnation stands fast in Plato's discourse, in that it is accepted by the other philosophers. Socrates' *reasoned argument* for the *immortality* of the soul also stands – but only in that the soul is 'un-dying', *not* in that it continues after death.[275]

The nature of 'the soul' as a continuous surviving entity that *transmigrates* from one incarnation to the next is still not established as a consequence of its immortality. This is never satisfactorily confirmed outside the context of mythical discourse.

This state of affairs has then been patched together by Plato's interpreters into a scenario in which Socrates is supposed to believe souls circulate intact in and out of bodies in a manner akin to taking the Myth of Er quite literally, rather than understanding the metaphor.

Conclusion

The role of Number and quantification in the idea of *the harmony of the spheres*, is essentially metaphysical, and metaphorical, and not proto-scientific. It sows the seed of what later becomes our scientific discovery of the relationship between Number and quantification, and the behaviour of what exists in nature, but it is not in itself, mistaken proto-science.

Like all Myths, the Myth of Er can be considered as an example of what Schopenhauer called a 'comprehensible substitute for the truth'. Every element in the story is a mythical symbol.

In particular, the myth as Socrates tells it appears to be a scenario of *metempsychosis* – the transmigration of the 'soul' from incarnation, through a process between incarnations, and back again into incarnation.

Thus, in the scenario as it appears, there is a self-entity, the 'soul' that *survives* throughout the process. The elements of the story dealing with this correspond with the general principle of the Buddhist and Hindu religions, in which life and death are cyclic. The doctrine of reincarnation as it is widely understood allows for this survival of self as 'soul', the form of each life being determined by the actions in the previous life.

As Schopenhauer perceptively recognised, the notion of ultimate self survival in the doctrine of reincarnation, is itself, like any doctrine, also supposed to be a comprehensible substitute for the truth, all the more appealing because it promises self survival.

The Myth of Er is in the class of the general doctrine of reincarnation, which Schopenhauer adequately addresses. The doctrine of reincarnation as the transmigration of a surviving self from one incarnation to the next, can be understood as merely a simple conceptual representation of a process in which reincarnation, as Schopenhauer puts it, is really through a *psychical* version of *palengenisis*.

In biological palengenisis no individual self survives – the species which we say survives, is a concept whose reality in matter at any time is only through the physical individual members who ultimately *do not survive*. The reality of 'the species' outside material form, is abstract.

Only in as much as a member's *identity* is with the abstract thing called *the species* does that member 'survive'. No individual member passes from death to birth, but births continue to arise.

By analogy, in reincarnation, only in as much as the identity of a 'soul' is not with a given 'incarnation', but with the great process in which nothing 'survives', governed by *harmonia* and the Fates, does the notion of 'survival' in continual incarnations, have any meaning.

To put it another way, only when a soul enjoys a state of consciousness in which nothing survives, and in which reincarnation is obvious, but an illusion, does reincarnation have any truth in it. Where there is no such consciousness, there is only the *notion* of survival from one birth to the next, and no truth in it.

This brings us to our conclusion about the mythology, and entire tradition of the harmony of the spheres. Just as today, there are those who take a subject-oriented view of life and the universe, and those who take an object-oriented view, so this was just as much the case at the time of the attestations.

Confusion always arises when the expression of one is interpreted through the eyes of the other, and then repeated, commented on, or echoed. This is a situation that exists in the attestations, and it is also often encountered today. Pythagoras, either as the originator of the tradition, or as the earliest known transmitter of it, even today is thought of by some as an early scientist, and by others, as a magus or spiritual teacher.

Plato faithfully represented the tradition in his own way, passing it on through *Timaeus* and the *Republic*. Plato's pupil, Aristotle, in contrast, took what was reported about the Pythagoreans quite literally and in an object-oriented way. Having created his own false target from the attestations, he then shot it down.

The reason the whole, generic idea of the harmony of the spheres still has something of an echo of truth about it for some people, even in the face of modern science, is precisely because of what lies behind its object-oriented appearance.

From the point of view of modern science, it has about the same status as astrology, to which it is of course, connected. But from the point of view of our subject-oriented experience as human beings, it addresses something that for many people is undeniable. And that is the power of music on our psyche.

What we can see is that the harmony of the spheres tradition actually rests on the early Greek idea of *harmonia*. This isn't simply something that pertains to practical music. It is a principle that "fits together" the limited things of our world, with the unlimited, or, what today, we might call the Infinite.

The Pythagorean Philolaus tells us that our understanding of nature is made by human intelligence, and that a true understanding of nature requires Divine intelligence. Human intelligence merely understands nature as existence. Whereas nature itself, is not what exists.

Plato explicitly describes *harmonia* operating in the cosmos in the *Republic*, and there, it is actually about reincarnation. The cosmos Plato describes there, is not the existing universe, as Philolaus would call it, but what Philolaus called *nature itself*. What Plato describes is a metaphor. And the implication is that those things that exist, the planets and stars, are themselves metaphors, because the whole of existence is the metaphor for nature itself.

In the context of the harmony of the spheres tradition, the essence of music in all its forms, is *harmonia*. Whether it is as practical music, *music practica*, or as human music, *musica humana*, which is the harmony in the human soul, or as the music of the spheres, *music mundana*. *Harmonia* is all about bringing the limited, that exists, into harmony with *the Infinite,* or *the One*, the Divine behind the appearance of existence.

In the end, music is a metaphor, and its powerful effect on our psyche, its power to order the soul, as Plato would have it, the very experience we have of it, is a metaphor for something higher. And the tradition, as a whole, is about the realisation of what the ancients called the One, the source of *harmonia* and the truth behind the much interpreted and misinterpreted idea of *harmonia mundi* - the harmony of the spheres.

References

[1] For a short synopsis on Heraclitus and Empidocles see Kassler, JC, *Inner Music*, London, 1995, pp. 30-33. Dates, and full translations of fragments relating to Heraclitus and Empidocles are in Diels, H, / Freeman, K (Tr.), *Ancilla to the Pre-Socratic Philosophers, A complete translation of the fragments in Diels,* Fragmente der Vorsokratiker, Oxford, 1971, pp. 24-34, and 51-69, respectively.

[2] Kassler, JC, *Inner Music*, London, 1995, pp. 31-32; Freeman, *Ancilla, op. cit.*, p. 28.

[3] Freeman, *Ancilla, op. cit.*, pp. 54-56. See also Kassler, JC, *Inner Music*, London, 1995, pp. 32.

[4] Philip, JA, *Pythagoras and early Pythagoreanism*, Toronto, 1966, p. 123.

[5] Lloyd, GER, *Polarity and Analogy - two types of argumentation in early Greek thought*, Cambridge, 1966, pp. 15-85.

[6] *Ibid.*

[7] Philip, JA, *Pythagoras and early Pythagoreanism*, Toronto, 1966, p. 47.

[8] Huffman, CA, *Philolaus of Croton*, Cambridge, 1993, p. 73.

[9] *Ibid.*, p. 328.

[10] Boethius, AMS, *Fundamentals of Music*, Tr. CM Bower, Ed. CV Palisca, New Haven & London, 1989, p. 9, cites seven primary sources that deal with the harmony of the heavens: Pliny, *Naturalis historia* 2.22(20).84; Cicero, *De republica* 6.18.18; Plutarch, *De musica* 1147; Nicomachus, *Enchiridion* 3; Censorinus, *De die natalai* 12; Macrobius, *In somnium Scipionis* 2.1.2 & 6.1-6; Ptolemy *Harmonica* 3.10-16 & 104-111. Schavernoch, H, *Die Harmonie der Sphären*, Munich, 1981, pp. 132-165 contains synopses of sixteen scholarly or philosophic works treating the subject of cosmic music or the harmony of the spheres, whose authors include Kepler, Fludd, Mersenne, Kircher, Newton, Leibniz, Kant, Schelling, Titus-Bode, Thomas Ring, Victor Goldschmidt, E. Zederbauer, August Boeckh, Wilhem Forester, von Thimus, and Rudolf Haase.
The literary works of twenty are treated, pp. 165-184, including the authors Sir Thomas Browne, Milton, Friedrich Gottlieb Klopstock, Gottfried August Bürger, Johann Gottfried Herder, Jakob Balde, Matthias Claudias, Goethe, Schiller, Hölderlin, Novalis, Brentano, Karoline von Gunderode, Joseph von Eichendorff, Heinriche Heine, Gottfried Keller, Proust, Gottfried Benn, and Hermann Hesse.
Also pp. 184-186 gives coverage of the attention paid to the harmony of the spheres by many composers and composer-theorists since Bardi's "L'Armonia della sfere" in the 1589 Intermedi. Included are Buxtehude and Hindemith. Moyer, AE, *Musica Scientia*, Ithaca & London, 1992, includes mention of Quintillian (p.28 ff., citing Quintillian, Marcus Fabius, *Institutio Oratorio*, Tr. HE Butler, London, 1921; *Quintillian's Institutes of Oratory*, Tr. JS Watson, {2 Vols}, London, 1903); Burtius (pp. 44 ff. & pp. 49-51, citing Burtius, Nicolaus, *Musices opusculum*, Tr. Clement A Miller, Musicological studies and documents 37, N.p.: American Institute of Musicology, 1983); Ramos de Pareja (p.52 ff.); Macrobius (p. 57); Martianus Capella (p. 57); Pliny (p.44); Tinctoris (p.65); Franchino Gaffurio (p. 73, & esp. pp. 86-9 on *De harmonia muiscorum instrumentroum opus*, Milan, 1518); Pietro Aron (p. 121); Tartaglia (p.131ff.); Luigi Dentice (p. 147); Cardano (p. 160); Zarlino (p. 207); Pietro Caetano (p. 265); Pietro Ponzio, Frate Angelo, Poliziano, Lefèvre d'Étaples, Plutarch, Celio Rodigino (all p. 271); Fabio Paolini (p. 274); Gentile Riccio

[11] Date taken from Diels, H, / Freeman, K (Tr.), *Ancilla to the Pre-Socratic Philosophers, A complete translation of the fragments in Diels,* Fragmente der Vorsokratiker, Oxford, 1971, p. 20.

[12] Huffman, CA, *Philolaus of Croton*, Cambridge, 1993, p. 57. The older Pythagoreans are Cercôps, Petrôn, Bro(n)tînus, Hippasos, Calliphôn and Dêmocêdês, Parm(en)iscus. Nothing certain is known of any written works: *vide* Freeman, *Ancilla, op. cit.*, p. 20. Accounts of Pythagoreanism derive mostly from the Peripatetic School (Aristoxenus, Theophrastus, Eudemus) and from the neo-Platonists (Porphyry, Iamblichus, Proclus, Simplicus). There are also extracts in the compilers (Diogenes Laertius, Stobaeus) and the lexicographers. But these accounts usually refer to the Pythagorean school rather than any particular member. *vide* Freeman, *Ancilla, op. cit.*, p. 82.

[13] c.f. Guthrie, WKC, *Orpheus and Greek religion*, London, 1935, p. 223. The idea that the soul in entombed in the body is also found in the Philolaus fragments (c. 500 BC). See Freeman, *Ancilla, op. cit.*, p. 74 (14).

[14] Taylor, T, *Iamblichus on the mysteries of the Egyptians, Chaldeans, and Assyrians*, London, 1821, pp. 133, 143.

[15] Maula, E, 'The conquest of time', *Diotima*, Vol. 11, 1983 p. 130.

[16] Philip, JA, *Pythagoras and early Pythagoreanism*, Toronto, 1966, p. 126.

[17] Plato, *The Republic*, 616b - 617d, Tr. D Lee, London, 1955, 1987, pp. 388-393.

[18] Plato, *Timaeus*, 34-37, esp. 35a-36d, in *Timaeus and Critias*, Tr. D Lee, London, 1965, 1977, p. 46-49.

[19] *Phaedrus*, 246, E-247 C, see Heath, Sir Thomas L, *Greek Astronomy*, New York (originally London), 1932, 1991, pp. 42-43.

[20] *Laws*, 889B-C. The concept of harmony, harmonic proportion, or concord, also appears in *Symposium*, 188A, and *Timaeus*, 32C (in relation to the elements), and in *Symposium* 188A, in relation to the seasons. (Also cited in Boethius, AMS, *Fundamentals of Music*, Tr. CM Bower, Ed. CV Palisca, New Haven & London, 1989, p. 9, notes).

21 The philological studies of the Myth consulted are given in Halliwell, S, *Plato: Republic 10*, Wiltshire, 1988, pp. 92 ff, & Richardson, H, 'The Myth of Er (Plato, *Republic*, 616B)', *CQ*, 20, 1926, pp. 113-133. Also consulted: Godwin, J, *Music, Mysticism and Magic*, London, 1986, pp. 3-8; notes pp. 295-299.

22 See also Lee, op. cit., p. 388; Halliwell, *op. cit*, p. 93; Stewart, JA, *The Myths of Plato*, London, 1960, p. 148; Richardson, *op. cit.*, p. 114.

23 Stewart, *op. cit.*, p. 150. Lee, Richardson, and Halliwell use a lower case 's' in 'Spindle'. Taylor, T, *The works of Plato*, London, 1804, Vol.1, pp. 466-475, reproduced in Godwin, *Music, Mysticism and Magic, op. cit.*, pp. 4-8, = 'distaff of necessity'.

24 Lee, *op. cit.*, pp. 400-404.

25 Lee, *op. cit.*, pp. 388-389; pp. 402-404.

26 Lee & Stewart, *op. cit.*; Taylor, *op. cit.* = [on] 'the knees of necessity' (This is the lit. tr. - See Halliwell, p. 181).

27 Lee gives 'siren' without capitalisation. Halliwell, p. 181, describes Sirens as often allegorically treated.

28 Lee refers to a 'constant pitch'; Halliwell refers to a 'single note'; Stewart refers to 'one pitch'; Taylor refers to 'diverse modulations'.

29 Lee suggests eight notes making up a single scale'; Halliwell refers to 'a unitary concord'; Stewart refers to 'one melody'; Taylor refers to 'one harmony' of eight notes. Halliwell, *op. cit.*, p. 94 refers to *harmonia*, the meaning of which is dealt with below.

30 The godesses of fate, in Halliwell only, *op. cit.*, p. 94; 95; 182.

31 Lee, *op. cit.* & Stewart *op. cit.*; Taylor says they have crowns on their heads; Halliwell refers to wreaths.

32 Halliwell states they are seated around the rim at equal intervals; Taylor says they are an equal distance from one another'; Stewart says they are at equal distances apart.

[33] Lee refers to the siren's music; Taylor refers to the harmony of the Sirens; Stewart refers to chanting to the melody of the Sirens; Halliwell refers to accompanying the Siren's concord'; Halliwell, p. 94, refers to *harmonia*.

[34] Lee, *op. cit.*; Taylor = 'daemon'; Stewart = 'Angel'; Halliwell = 'daimon'.

[35] See, for example, Maula, E, 'The conquest of Time', *Diotima*, Vol. 11, 1983, pp. 130-148.

[36] Halliwell, *op. cit.*, p. 93.

[37] Halliwell, *op. cit.*, p. 180.

[38] See Plato, *Timeaus*, Tr. Lee, *op. cit.*, p. 47 & frontispiece.

[39] *Timeaus*, Tr. Lee, *op. cit.*, p. 48.

[40] A large whole tone.

[41] The ratio of 256/243 which also appears in Eratosthenes' Diatonic tuning and Ptolemy's Diatonic Diatoniaion. See Murray Barbour, J, *Tuning and Temperament*, New York (originally Michigan), 1951, 1972, pp. 19-21.

[42] Cornford, FM, *Plato's Cosmology*, London, 1937, p. 68.

[43] Levin, FR, *The harmonics of Nicomachus and the Pythagorean tradition*, Pennsylvania, 1975. p.1.

[44] *Ibid.*, p. 69.

[45] *De Caelo*, II, 9, 289a 11-291b 23; Tr. in Heath, Sir Thomas L, *Greek Astronomy*, New York, (originally London) 1932, 1991, p. 73 ff.

[46] O'Neal, *Early astronomy from Babylonia to Copernicus*, Sydney, 1986, p. 61 ff; see also Heath, *Greek Astronomy*, *op. cit.*, pp. xliv ff.

[47] *Ibid.*, p. 65 ff.

[48] *Metaphysics*, 8, 1073 a 23-b 17, Tr. in Heath, Sir Thomas L, *Greek Astronomy*, London 1932, pp. 72-73.

[49] Heath, *Greek Astronomy*, *op. cit.*, p. 79.

[50] *Ibid.*, p. 11.

[51] *Ibid.*, p. 79.

[52] *Metaphysics*, Book Alpha, 985b ff, cited in Moyer, AE, *Musica Scientia*, Ithaca & London, 1992, p. 19.

[53] *Metaphysics*, A 5, 986, a 1; Heath, *Greek Astronomy*, *op. cit.*, p. 34.

[54] Philip, JA, *Pythagoras and early Pythagoreanism*, Toronto, 1966, pp. 123-124; Translation of Alexander's description of the doctrine, (*Metaphysics*, A 5, p. 542 a 5-18 Brandis) appears in Heath, Sir Thomas L, *Greek Astronomy*, New York, (originally London) 1932, 1991, pp. 34-35.

[55] Huffman, CA, *Philolaus of Croton*, Cambridge, 1993, p. 280.

[56] Burkert, W, *Lore and science in ancient Pythagoreanism*, Cambridge, 1972, pp. 353-354.

[57] Clark, G, *Iamblichus: On the Pythagorean Life*, Liverpool, 1989, pp. 85-86.

[58] 'The notorious "three books", bought for one hundred minai, at a time when Philolaus was desperately poor', *Ibid.*

[59] *De Caelo*, B 13, 293 a 15-b 30; Tr. Heath, *Greek Astronomy*, *op. cit.*, pp. 30-31; Also Heath, *Aristarchus*, *op. cit.*, p.96.

[60] *De Caelo*, II, 9, see Plato, Tr, Lee, *op. cit.*, p. 400; *Metaphysics*, $\Lambda 8$, see Heath, *Greek Astronomy*, *op. cit.*, p. 78.

[61] The counter-earth was said to be invisible because it was continuously obscured from sight.

[62] *Metaphysics*, A 5, 985 a 1; Tr. Heath, *Greek Astronomy*, *op. cit.*, p. 34.

[63] c.f. Kingsley, P, *Ancient philosophy, mystery and magic*, Oxford, 1995, p. 174.

[64] Burkert, W, *Lore and science in ancient Pythagoreanism*, Cambridge, Massachusetts, 1972, p. 353.

[65] Aëtius, II, 7, 7, (Diels, revised by Kranz, A16), Explicitly mentions the sun as one of the 'divine bodies' that move in a 'dance' around the 'middle'. See Tr. Heath, *Greek Astronomy, op. cit.*, pp. 32-33; Tr, Huffman, *Philolaus, op. cit.*, pp. 237-238; Aëtius, III, 13, 2, (Diels, revised by Kranz, A21).

[66] Philip, JA, *Pythagoras and early Pythagoreanism*, Toronto, 1966, pp. 113-114, states that Simplicus reports Philolaus to have held 'The middle is first in rank. Around it move in choral dance ten divine bodies: the sphere of fixed stars, the five planets, sun, moon, earth, and counter-earth'.

[67] Huffman, *Philolaus of Croton, op. cit.*, pp. 231-240, cites other attestations to the astronomical system of Philolaus: Aristotle, *De Caelo*, 2.3, 293a18ff; *Metaph.* 38.20, *De Caelo* 511.25, Simplicus, *Ph.* 1354.2, Diels, revised by Kranz, (DK) A16 (=Aetius 2.7.7), DK A17 (=Aetius 3.11.3), DK A21 (=Aetius 3.13.2), Eudemus, F146(=Simplicus, *De Caelo* 471.4 = DK 12A19), Aristotle, *Met.* 342b30 & 345a14.

[68] Heath, Sir Thomas L, *Aristarchus of Samos - the ancient Greek Copernicus*, Oxford, 1913, 1959, p. 107 ff.

[69] Huffman, CA, *Philolaus of Croton, op. cit.*, p. 240.

[70] *Ibid.*, p. 281.

[71] *Ibid.*, p. 59; see also p. 202.

[72] Burkert, Walter, *Lore and science in ancient Pythagoreanism*, Cambridge, Massachusetts, 1972, p. 352.

[73] *Ibid.*, p. 357.

[74] *Ibid.*, p. 355; & cited in Huffman, *Philolaus of Croton, op. cit.*, p. 279.

75 For a tr. of Nicomachus' account in *Enchiridion* 6, see Levin, FR, *The harmonics of Nicomachus and the Pythagorean tradition*, Pennsylvania, 1975, p. 70. For a tr. of Iamblichus' account see Clark, G, *Iamblichus: On the Pythagorean Life*, Liverpool, 1989, pp. 50-54. For citations of other sources see Levin, FR, *The harmonics of Nicomachus and the Pythagorean tradition*, Pennsylvania, 1975, p. 70 ff.

76 The story occurs in numerous other sources and asserts that Pythagoras found the weights of the hammers to be in the ratios 6:8:9:12, and confirmed his findings by hanging weights in the same ratios on tensioned strings of fixed length. The ratios would only produce the musical intervals of a fourth, fifth, and octave, when applied as linear divisions of the length of a tensioned string, not when applied to the weights or tension in the string.

77 Levin, *op. cit.*, p. 6.

78 AE Taylor, *A Commentary on Plato's Timaeus*, Oxford, 1928, pp. 164 & 489. Cited in Levin, *op. cit.*, p. 67.

79 Heath, *Aristarchus, op. cit.*, p. 46. Cited in Levin, *op. cit.*, p. 67.

80 A Delatte, *Etudes sur la litterature Pythagoricienne*, Paris, 1915, p. 259. Cited in Levin, *op. cit.*, p. 68.

81 Philip, JA, *Pythagoras and early Pythagoreanism*, Toronto, 1996, p. 126.

82 *Ibid.*, p. 128.

83 Burkert, *Lore and science, op. cit.*, p. 351.

84 Boethius, AMS, *Fundamentals of Music*, Tr. CM Bower, Ed. CV Palisca, New Haven & London, 1989, p. 29.

85 Levin, *op. cit.*, p. 75.

86 Ptolemy's system (late 1st or early 2nd century AD) was, however, heavily indebted to Hipparchus (BC c.190-c.120).

[87] Taub, LC, *Ptolemy's universe*, Chicago & LaSalle, Illinois, 1993, pp. 125-126; Barker, A, *Greek musical writings*, Vol.2, Cambridge, 1989, p. 278. On the *kanon*, see Barker, *op. cit.*, pp. 278; 291; 319; 340-345; 362 ff.

[88] Levin, *op. cit.*, p. 101.

[89] *Ibid.*, pp. 69-70.

[90] Kahn, CH, *Anaximander and the origins of Greek cosmology*, New York, 1960, p. 95.

[91] Pseudo-Plutarch, *Stromat* 2. See Heath, *Greek Astronomy, op. cit.*, p. 5; Kahn, *Anaximander, op. cit.*, p. 85; Conche, M, *Anaximandre - Fragments et Témoignagnes*, Paris, 1991, p. 193.

[92] Aëtius, II, 13, 7; 20,1; 21, 1; 24, 2; 25, 1 29, 1. Tr. Heath, *Greek Astronomy, op. cit.*, pp. 5-7; Hippolytus, *Refutation of all Heresies*, I, 6, 4, 5. Tr. Heath, *Greek Astronomy, op. cit.*, p. 5. See also Kahn, *Anaximander, op. cit.*, pp. 85, 87.

[93] Aëtius, II, 11, 2. Tr. Heath, *Greek Astronomy, op. cit.*, p. 21.

[94] Hippolytus & Pseudo-Plutarch, *op. cit.*, Tr. Heath, *Greek Astronomy, op. cit.*, p. 6; See also Kahn, *Anaximander, op. cit.*, p. 81.

[95] Conche, M, *Anaximandre - Fragments et Témoignagnes*, Paris, 1991, p. 209.

[96] Hippolytus, *Refutation of all Heresies*, I, 6, 5. Tr. Heath, *Greek Astronomy, op. cit.*, p. 6. See also Kahn, *Anaximander, op. cit.*, p. 85.

[97] Aëtius, II, 20, 1. Tr. Heath, *Greek Astronomy, op. cit.*, p. 6.

[98] *Ibid.*

[99] Aëtius, II, 25, 1. Tr. Heath, *Greek Astronomy, op. cit.*, pp. 6-7.

[100] Aëtius, II, 15, 6. Tr. Heath, *Greek Astronomy, op. cit.*, p. 7.

[101] See, for example, Conche, M, *Anaximandre - Fragments et Témoignagnes*, Paris, 1991, p. 209. An interpretation that fits the statements consistently is:

a) The diameter across the centre of the celestial system, of the circle that runs along the centre of the ring of fire, is 28 the diameter of the Earth.

b) The width or diameter of the fire itself, which is the same as the width of the hollow in the air enclosing it, is the same as the diameter of the Earth.

c) The diameter across the centre of the celestial system, of the line along the surface of the hollow containing the fire, that is closest to the centre of the celestial system, is 27 times the diameter of the Earth.

[102] Huffman, *Philolaus, op. cit.*, p. 58.

[103] *Fragmente der Vorsokratiker.*

[104] Freeman, *Ancilla, op. cit.*, p. 78.

[105] *Ibid.*, p. 78.

[106] *Ibid.*, p. 79-80.

[107] *Ibid.*, p. 80-81. The argument in favour of arithmetic seems to be in refutation of the notion that geometry is superior, a belief that arises because of its ability to deal with functions that involve the irrational proportions that simple arithmetic is unable to express, without the aid of decimal convention.

[108] *Ibid.*, pp. 73-77.

[109] Kahn, *Anaximander, op. cit.*, p. 95.

[110] *Ibid.*, p. 97.

[111] Dicks, DR, *Early Greek astronomy to Aristotle*, London, 1970, p. 45.

[112] Kahn, *Anaximander, op. cit.*, pp. 95-96.

[113] Heath, Sir Thomas, *Aristarchus, op. cit.*, p. 38.

[114] Kahn, *Anaximander, op. cit.*, p. 95.

[115] *Ibid.*, p. 96.

[116] *Ibid.*

[117] I have no reason to doubt the scholarship of the translators to whose work I make reference, all of whom are cited here.

[118] Freeman, *Ancilla*, p. 74.

[119] *Ibid.*

[120] Kirk, GS; Raven, JE; Schofield, M, *the pre-Socratic philosophers*, Cambridge, 1983, pp. 73-74.

[121] Guthrie, WKC, *Orpheus and Greek religion*, London, 1935, p. 1.

[122] Kirk, Raven and Schofield, *op. cit.*, p. 221.

[123] Guthrie, WKC, *Orpheus and Greek religion*, London, 1935, p. 220.

[124] *Ibid.*, p. 217.

[125] *Ibid.*, p. 219.

[126] *Ibid.*, p. 220.

[127] *Ibid.*, p. 218.

[128] *Ibid.*, p. 219.

[129] Claudianus Mamertus purporting to be quoting from the third volume of Philolaus' *On rhythm and metre*. See Freeman, *Ancilla, op. cit.*, p. 77.

[130] Ancilla, *ibid.*, p. 73.

[131] *Ibid.*, p.74.

[132] *Ibid.*, p.74.

[133] See, for example, Rattansi, PM, 'Art and Science: The Paracelsian Vision', *Science and the Arts in the Renaissance*, Ed. John W Shirley & F David Hoeniger, 3, pp. 50 – 57.

[134] *Harmonics*, Book III, Ch. 4; Barker, A, *Greek musical writings*, (2 Vols), Cambridge, 1989, Vol. 2, pp. 375-376.

[135] Taylor, T, *Iamblichus on the mysteries of the Egyptians, Chaldeans, and Assyrians*, London, 1821, 1968, pp. 133, 143.

[136] Cornford, FM, 'The unconscious element in literature and philosophy', *The Unwritten Philosophy and other essays*, Cambridge, 1967, p. 19.

[137] See Dillon, J and Hershbell, J, *Iamblichus On the Pythagorean Way of Life*, Atlanta, Georgia, 1991, pp. 89-91. The idea is perhaps traceable to Nicomachus - Porphyry's Life of Pythagoras, 30, claims Nicomachus to have stated that Pythagoras had the gift of hearing the music of the spheres, see Chadwick, H, *Boethius - The consolations of music, logic, theology, and philosophy*, Oxford, 1981, 1990.

[138] *Ibid.*

[139] See, as probably one of the earliest examples, Bywater, I, 'On the fragments attributed to Philolaus', *Journal of Philology*, Vol.1, 1868, pp. 20-53.

[140] Freeman, *Ancilla, op. cit.*, p. 73.

[141] Huffman, CA, *Philolaus of Croton*, Cambridge, 1993, p. 59.

[142] Freeman, *Ancilla, Ibid.*, p. 74.

[143] *Ibid.*, p. 75. A fifth element is also mentioned, the δλκός of the 'Sphere'.

[144] *Ibid.*

[145] *Ibid.*, p. 75.

[146] *Ibid.*

[147] *Ibid.*, p. 74.

[148] *Ibid.*, p. 74.

[149] *Ibid.*

[150] *Ibid.*, p. 74.

[151] *Ibid.*, p. 75.

[152] *Ibid.*, p. 75.

[153] *Ibid.*, p. 75

[154] Freeman, *Ancilla, op. cit.*, p. 77.

[155] *Ibid.*, p. 73.

[156] *Ibid.*

[157] *Ibid.*, p. 76.

[158] In the broadest modern sense, this means the intelligence arising in the brain and body of the human animal.

[159] Freeman, *Ancilla, op. cit.*, p. 77.

[160] *Ibid.*, p. 74.

[161] Huffman, CA, *Philolaus of Croton*, Cambridge, 1993, p. 410.

[162] Philip, JA, *Pythagoras and early Pythagoreanism*, Toronto, 1966, pp. 113-114.

[163] Huffman, CA, *Philolaus of Croton, op. cit.*, p. 243.

[164] Freeman, *Ancilla, op. cit.*, p. 74.

[165] Philip, JA, *Pythagoras and early Pythagoreanism, op. cit.*, pp. 113-114; Huffman, *Philolaus, op. cit.*, pp. 237-238; Diels (revised by Kranz) A16 (=Aetius 2.7.7).

[166] Huffman, CA, *Philolaus of Croton, op.cit.*, p. 411; Freeman, *Ancilla, op. cit.*, p. 77.

[167] Aëtius in: 2.20.12; Diels, 348. Achilles in: *Isagoga excerpta* 19; Maas 46.13 (cited in Huffman, *Philolaus, op. cit.*, pp. 266, 267, respectively). Achilles appears in Diels, H, *Doxographi Graeci*, Berlin, 1874, pp. 349, 350.

[168] Heath, *Aristarchus, op. cit.*, pp. 115-116.

169 Heath, *Aristarchus, op. cit.*, p. 116.

170 Aëtius, II, 20, 13. Heath, *Greek Astronomy, op. cit.*, p. 22.

171 Freeman, *Ancilla, op. cit.*, p. 64.

172 Freeman, *Ancilla, op. cit.*, p. 58.

173 Plutarch, *De Pyth. Or.*, 12, p. 400 B. Heath, *Greek Astronomy, op. cit.*, p. 22.

174 Diels, H, *Doxographi Graeci*, Berlin, 1874, pp. 349, 350.

175 Dobbs, BJT, *The janus faces of genius. The role of alchemy in Newton's thought*, Cambridge, 1991, p. 158.

176 Huffman, WH, *Robert Fludd and the end of the renaissance*, London, 1988, p. 94 ff.

177 Dobbs, BJT, *The janus faces of genius. The role of alchemy in Newton's thought*, Cambridge, 1991, p. 159; citing Gombrich, EH, *Symbolic Images. Studies in the Art of the Renaissance, with 170 Illustrations. II.*, Chicago, 1972, 1985, pp. 152-153.

178 Plato, *The Republic* 507e - 509c; See Plato, *The Republic*, Tr. D Lee, London, 1955, 1987, pp. 245-255.

179 Dobbs, BJT, *The janus faces of genius, op. cit.*, p. 157.

180 *Ibid.*

181 *Ibid.*, p. 161;
Yates, FA, *Giordano Bruno and the Hermetic Tradition*, Chicago, London & Toronto, 1964, pp. 7-9, 23, 36.

182 An example is the work of the Spanish mystic St John of the Cross, perhaps best known for his treatise *Dark Night of the Soul*. For a short example, see, in particular, St. John of the Cross, *Living Flame of Love*, Tr. EA Peers, Tunbridge Wells, 1935, 1987, pp. 127-130.

183 See Kristeller, PO, *Eight philosophers of the Italian renaissance*, Stanford, 1966, pp. 120-121.

[184] Kristeller, PO, *The philosophy of Marsilio Ficino*, Tr. V Conant, Columbia, 1943, p. 127.

[185] *Ibid.*, p. 98; Also partially cited in Dobbs, BJT, *The janus faces of genius. The role of alchemy in Newton's thought, op. cit.*, p. 159 (n.113).

[186] French, P, *John Dee*, London, 1987, pp. 94-96.

[187] On Kepler and the Hermetic philosophy see Field, DIV, *Kepler's geometrical cosmology*, London, 1943, 1988, pp. 187-190.

[188] *Opera Omni*, Vol. IX, pp. 33 ff. 5; see Kestrel, A, *The act of creation*, London, 1964, p. 125.

[189] Kingsley, *op. cit.*, p. 53, states that there is a nexus of Greek passages alluding to the idea that the fires of heaven, including the sun, had their origin in the depths of the Earth.

[190] Kingsley, *op. cit.*, pp. 55-57.

[191] French, P, *John Dee*, London, 1987, p. 127; See also, for example, *ibid.* pp. 77-78 & footnotes, and Reedy, J, *Thomas Norton's Ordinal of Alchemy*, Oxford, 1975.

[192] Freeman, *Ancilla, op. cit.*, p. 28, footnote 1.

[193] Tr. Freeman as 'Law'. Literally, 'word'.

[194] Freeman, *Ancilla, op. cit.*, p. 28.

[195] *Ibid.*

[196] Philip, JA, *Pythagoras and early Pythagoreanism, op. cit.*, p. 127.

[197] e.g. Plato, *Timaeus and Critias*, 30-32, Tr. D Lee, 1965, 1977, p. 43.

[198] Combs, A, 'The meeting ground of science and spirit: New themes for a new science', in Burner. *et. al.* (Eds.), *Holistic Science and Human Values*, Adder (Theosophical Science Centre), Madras, 1992, pp. 53-59; cited in Bags, S & J, *The Healthy House*, London, 1996, p. 89.

[199] Attributed to Pythagoras, for example by Hippolytus in *Refutations*, I, 2, 2, see Heath, *Greek Astronomy, op. cit.*, p. 34.

[200] Solomon, J, *Harmony in Ptolemy's Harmonics*, Armadillo, NSW, 1990, p. 13.

[201] Taub, LC, *Ptolemy's universe*, Chicago & LaSalle, Illinois, 1993, p. 127; Barker, A, *Greek musical writings*, (2 Vols), Cambridge, 1989, Vol. 2, pp. 375-376.

[202] *Harmonics*, Book III, Chapters 4, 8-16; Barker, A, *Greek musical writings*, (2 Vols), Cambridge, 1989, Vol. 2, pp. 375-376; 380-391.

[203] Solomon, J, *Harmony in Ptolemy's Harmonics*, Armidale, NSW, 1990, p. 16.

[204] *Ibid.*, pp. 15-16.

[205] *Harmonics*, Book III, Ch. 4; Barker, A, *Greek musical writings*, (2 Vols), Cambridge, 1989, Vol. 2, p. 374.

[206] Huffman, WH, *Robert Fludd and the end of the renaissance*, London, 1988, p. 80.

[207] Moyer, AE, *Musica Scientia*, Ithaca & London, 1992, p. 29.

[208] Huffman, CA, *Philolaus of Croton*, Cambridge, 1993, p. 364.

[209] Moyer, AE, *Musica Scientia*, Ithaca & London, 1992, p. 29.

[210] *Ibid.*, p. 30.

[211] *Ibid.*, pp. 29-30; French, P, *John Dee*, London, 1987, p. 23.

[212] See, for example, Boethius, AMS, *Fundamentals of Music*, Tr. CM Bower, Ed. CV Palisca, New Haven & London, 1989, pp. 16-17, 50, 165.

[213] Moyer, AE, *Musica Scientia, op.* cit., pp. 100-103.

[214] *Ibid.*, p. 7.

[215] The *Hermetica* is now generally thought to be neo-Platonic in origin, even if ultimately derived from Egyptian teaching. Scott, W (Tr), *Hermetica*, (1924), Bath, 1992.

[216] French, *op.cit.*, p. 140.

[217] *Utriusque Cosmi....Historia,* 1617 - 1626. See Godwin, J, *Robert Fludd*, London, 1979; Huffman, WH, *Robert Fludd and the end of the renaissance*, London, 1988.

[218] For a concise overview of the Chain of Being, see Tillyard, EMW, *The Elizabethan World Picture*, London, 1943, 1972, p. 33 ff. The classic study is Lovejoy, AO, *The Great Chain of Being*, Cambridge, Mass., 1936.

[219] Tillyard, *op. cit.* For an illustrated overview of Fludd's macrocosm-microcosm cosmology see Godwin, J, *Robert Fludd*, London, 1979.

[220] French, *op. cit.*, pp. 139-140.

[221] Tillyard, *op. cit.*

[222] *Ibid.*, in particular pp. 49-50, 59, 96.

[223] Especially through Sir Philip Sidney and his circle. French, *op. cit.*, p. 126 ff.

[224] French, *op. cit.*, pp. 139-140.

[225] French, *op. cit.*, pp. 139-140.

[226] Kristeller, PO, *Eight philosophers of the Italian renaissance*, Stanford, 1966, pp. 42-43..

[227] Kristeller, PO, *The philosophy of Marsilio Ficino*, Tr. V Conant, Columbia, 1943, p. 307.

[228] French, *op. cit.*, p. 138.

[229] Lowinsky, EE, 'Music in the culture of the renaissance', in Kristeller, PO & Wiener, PP, *Renaissance Essays*, New York, 1968, 1992, p. 344.

119

[230] Ficino, M, *The Book of Life*, Tr. Charles Boer, Dallas, Texas, 1992, pp. 158-164.

[231] French, *op. cit.*, pp. 138; Godwin, J, *Music, mysticism and magic*, London, 1987, pp. 117-122.

[232] French, *ibid.*, p. 138.

Kristeller, PO, *The philosophy of Marsilio Ficino, op.cit.*, 1943, p. 308.

[233] *Ibid.*, pp. 74-120; p. 88 in particular.

[234] Boer, C, *Marsilio Ficino's Book of Life*, Dallas, 1992.

[235] Shorey, P, *Platonism Ancient and Modern*, Berkeley, 1938, p. 120.

[236] Kristeller, PO, *Eight philosophers of the Italian renaissance, op. cit*, 41-42.

[237] *Ibid.*, 51-52.

[238] *Ibid.*, pp. 54-71.

[239] Ficino, M, *The Book of Life, op. cit.*, pp. xi-xii.

[240] Kristeller, PO, *Eight philosophers of the Italian renaissance, op. cit.*, 37-53. For the commentary on *Symposium* see Jayne, SR, *Marsilio Ficino's commentary on Plato's Symposium*, Columbia, 1944. (Vol. 19 of University of Missouri Studies).

[241] The assertion that the Earth moves, and is not at the centre of the cosmos is at least as old as the cosmology of Philolaus.

[242] Descartes, R, *The philosophical writings of Descartes*, Tr. J Cottingham, R Stoothoff, D Murdoch, Cambridge, 1985, 1994, Vol. 1, p. 109 ff.

[243] Descartes, Tr. J Cottingham, R Stoothoff, D Murdoch, *op. cit.*, Vol. 1., pp. 210-216.

[244] This is well known in the history of science discipline, but for example, see Huffman, WH, *Robert Fludd and the end of the renaissance*, London, 1988, p. 56.

[245] See Godwin, J, *Music, mysticism and magic, op. cit.*, pp. 148-152.

[246] Godwin, J, *Harmonies of Heaven and Earth*, London, 1987, pp. 143-148; Walker, DP, *studies in musical science in the late renaissance*, London, 1978, pp. 34-62.

[247] Asimov, I, *Biographical encyclopedia of science and technology*, London, 1972, p. 139.

[248] *Ibid.*

[249] Kassler, JC, *Inner Music: Hobbes, Hooke and North on Internal Character*, London, 1995.

[250] Bacon, F, *The advancement of learning*, 1605, Ed. A Johnston, Oxford, 1986, p. 106; cited in Kassler, *op. cit.*, p. 211.

[251] Kassler, *op. cit.*, p. 231.

[252] Damasio, A, *Descartes' Error*, New York, 1994, London, 1996, p. 257.

[253] These medical writers were not theorists, but invariably practising physicians. Scientific lecturing was based mainly on the work of London entrepreneurs, whereas medical lecturing primarily had a vocational aim. See Porter, R, 'Medical lecturing in Georgian London', *British Journal for the History of Science*, 1995, 28, pp. 91-99.

[254] In particular, Browne, Richard, *Medicina Musica or, a Mechanical Essay on the Effects of Singing, Musick, and Dancing, on Human Bodies....*, London, 1729; Brocklesby, Richard, *Reflections on Ancient and Modern Musick, with the Application to the Cure of Diseases....*, London, 1749.

[255] Browne, Richard, *Medicina Musica, op. cit.*; Brocklesby, Richard, *Reflections, op. cit.*, Ch. 4, p. 45 ff.; Elliot, Sir John Bart, *Elements of the branches of natural philosophy connected with medicine*, London, 1786, Ch. XIV, p. 259, especially p. 260 ff.

[256] See, for example, Adair, James Makittrick, *A philosophical and medical sketch of the natural history of the human body and mind. To which is subjoined, an essay on the difficulties of attaining medical knowledge.*, Bath, 1787, p. 40; pp. 94-96;

Buchan, William, *Domestic medicine: or, A treatise on the prevention and cure of diseases. 11th ed.*, London, 1790, pp. 60; 111-121; 428; Cogan, Thomas, *A philosophical treatise on the passions*, Bath, 1800, pp. 278-298;

Duncan, Andrew, 'Observations respecting the use of music in cases of melancholia', *Heads of lectures on the theory and practice of medicine. 4th ed., corrected*, Edinburgh, 1790, p. 180;

Gregory, John, *A Comparative View of the State & Faculties of Man with those of the Animal World*, London, 1765, p. 6.;

Gregory, John, *Lectures on the Duties and Qualifications of a Physician*, London, 1772, p. 165;

Mead, Richard, *The Medical Works of Richard Mead*, Edinburgh, 1792, ch. XVIII, pp. 425-428.

257 Crudely speaking, vitalism held that living organisms were differentiated from inanimate matter by the presence of 'vital' or 'animal spirit', a mysterious 'substance' or 'fluid' that with some kind of connection to 'the soul', was responsible for a range of phenomena in the human organism, including movement and emotion. Much of the thinking relating to this paradigm derives from Descartes.

It was opposed by the mechanical philosophers, but Bryan Robinson, in 1732, described the notions of vitalism as 'received opinion'. See Robinson, B, Robinson, Bryan, *A treatise of the animal eoconomy*, Dublin, 1732, p. 84.

On vitalism and the notion of vital or animal 'spirit' in the philosophy of organism, see Myers, CS, 'Vitalism: A Brief Historical and Critical Review', *Mind*, Vol.9, 1900, pp. 218-233; 319-331; Sutton, G, 'The Physical and Chemical Path to Vitalism: Xavier Bichat's *Physiological researches on Life and Death*', *Bulletin of the History of Medicine*, Vol.58, Spring 1984, No.1, pp. 53-71;

Melzer, SJ, 'Vitalism and Mechanism in Biology and Medicine', *Science*, Vol.XIX, No.470, 1904, pp. 18-22;

Haller, JS Jnr, 'The Great Biological Problem: Vitalism, materialism, and the philosophy of organism', *New York State Journal of Medicine*, Vol.86, No.2, February 1986, pp. 81-88.

258 See Clark, G, *Iamblichus: On the Pythagorean Life*, Liverpool, 1989, pp. 48-49; Dillon, J, & Hershbell, J, *Iamblichus on the Pythagorean Way of Life*, Atlanta, Georgia, 1991, p. 89.

259 Godwin, J, *Harmonies of Heaven and Earth*, London, 1987, p. 167.

260 A limited commentary appears in James, J, *The music of the spheres: music, science, and the natural order of the universe*, London, 1995, pp. 219-220; 225-228.

261 Combarieu, J, *Histoire de la musique des origines au début du Xx^me siècle*, Paris, 1913-1930. See Dwight Allen, *Philosophies of Music History*, New York, 1939, 1962, pp. 187-189.

262 For surveys see Godwin, J, *Harmonies of Heaven and Earth*, London, 1987; Godwin, J, *Music, mysticism and magic*, London, 1987; James, J, *The music of the spheres: music, science, and the natural order of the universe*, London, 1995, especially pp. 219-220, & 225-228.

263 Surveys can be found in Godwin, J, *Robert Fludd Hermetic philosopher and surveyor of two worlds*, London, 1979, and Purce, J, *The Mystic Spiral*, London, 1974, 1980.

264 'Like' mathematics in appearance, or inclusive of some mathematics, but not really the science of mathematics itself.

265 The harmonic ratio of a musical interval is the integer ratios corresponding to the ratios of the fundamental frequencies of the notes forming the interval. Traditionally the ratios were expressed as the ratios of the string lengths of a monochord required to produce the interval.

266 In the science of *harmonics* the 'direction', ascending or descending, of an interval, is merely relative. Intervals and their associated ratios can be handled in any way according to chosen convention. A fourth is merely an inverted fifth and *vice versa*, a major third is an inverted minor sixth, etc. Consequently the Circle can equally represent alternating ascending fifths and descending fourths, clockwise, and descending fifths and ascending fourths, anticlockwise. The entire Circle then represents a scale of twelve tones in one octave.

267 A comma is a microtonal interval. The Pythagorean comma is also called the ditonic comma.

268 It 'howls' unpleasantly 'out of tune'.

269 The difference between these thirds and true harmonic major thirds is the difference between the syntonic and ditonic (Pythagorean) commas – about 2 cents, or a 50th of a semitone.

270 Equal temperament, as a proposed system of tuning, is not a modern idea, but its adoption as a 'universal' standard is modern.

271 For example, Vicentino's 31 note Equal Temperament, Vicentino, Nicola, *L'antica musica ridotta alla moderna prattica*, Rome, 1555.

124

272 For this chapter, cf. Plato, Phaedo 84a – 95a, Plato, *The Last Days of Socrates*, Tr. H Tredennick and H Tarrant, London, 1954, 1993, pp. 143 –157.

273 *Ibid.*, 93b-c.

274 *Ibid.*, 93c-d.

275 *Ibid.*, 100b-106a, pp. 163 – 172 and Phaedo 107e-d.

Bibliography

Includes sources cited in the text and those
consulted in the original research

Adair, James Makittrick, *A philosophical and medical sketch of the natural history of the human body and mind. To which is subjoined, an essay on the difficulties of attaining medical knowledge.*, Bath, 1787

Allen, W Dwight, *Philosophies of Music History*, New York, 1939, 1962

Asimov, I, *Biographical encyclopedia of science and technology*, London, 1972

Bacon, F, *The advancement of learning*, 1605, Ed. A Johnston, Oxford, 1986

Bags, S & J, *The Healthy House*, London, 1996

Barker, A, *Greek musical writings*, (2 Vols), Cambridge, 1989

Boethius, AMS, *Fundamentals of Music*, Tr. CM Bower, Ed. CV Palisca, New Haven & London, 1989

Bohm, D, *Wholeness and the Implicate Order*, London, 1980

Brocklesby, Richard, *Reflections on Ancient and Modern Musick, with the Application to the Cure of Diseases....*, London, 1749

Brockman, J & Rosenfield, E, *Real Time*, London, 1973

Browne, Richard, *Medicina Musica or, a Mechanical Essay on the Effects of Singing, Musick, and Dancing, on Human Bodies....*, London, 1729

Buchan, William, *Domestic medicine: or, A treatise on the prevention and cure of diseases.* 11th ed., London, 1790

Budd, M, *Music and the Emotions*, London, 1985

Burkert, W, *Lore and science in ancient Pythagoreanism*, Cambridge, Massachusetts, 1972

Bywater, I, 'On the fragments attributed to Philolaus', *Journal of Philology*, Vol.1, 1868

Clark, G, *Iamblichus: On the Pythagorean Life*, Liverpool, 1989

Cogan, Thomas, *A philosophical treatise on the passions*, Bath, 1800

Combarieu, J, *Histoire de la musique des origines au début du Xx^me siècle*, Paris, 1913-1930

Combs, A, 'The meeting ground of science and spirit: New themes for a new science', in Burner. *et. al.* (Eds.), *Holistic Science and Human Values*, Adder (Theosophical Science Centre), Madras, 1992

Conche, M, *Anaximandre - Fragments et Témoignagnes*, Paris, 1991

Cornford, FM, 'The unconscious element in literature and philosophy', Cornford, FM; Guthrie, WKC, *The unwritten philosophy and other essays*, Oxford, 1950

Cornford, FM, *Plato's Cosmology*, London, 1937

Damasio, A, *Descartes' Error*, New York, 1994, London, 1996

Davies, PCW and Brown, JR (Eds.), *The Ghost in the Atom*, Cambridge, 1986

Davies, JD; Hersh, R, *The Mathematical Experience*, Middlesex, UK, 1981

Delatte, A, *Etudes sur la litterature Pythagoricienne*, Paris, 1915

Descartes, R, *The philosophical writings of Descartes*, Tr. J Cottingham, R Stoothoff, D Murdoch, Cambridge, 1985, 1994

Dicks, DR, *Early Greek astronomy to Aristotle*, London, 1970

Diels, H, / Freeman, K (Tr.), *Ancilla to the Pre-Socratic Philosophers, A complete translation of the fragments in Diels,* Fragmente der Vorsokratiker, Oxford, 1948

Diels, H, *Doxographi Graeci*, Berlin, 1874

Dillon, J and Hershbell, J, *Iamblichus On the Pythagorean Way of Life*, Atlanta, Georgia, 1991

Dobbs, BJT, *The janus faces of genius. The role of alchemy in Newton's thought*, Cambridge, 1991

Duncan, Andrew, 'Observations respecting the use of music in cases of melancholia', *Heads of lectures on the theory and practice of medicine. 4th ed., corrected*, Edinburgh, 1790

Elliot, Sir John Bart, *Elements of the branches of natural philosophy connected with medicine*, London, 1786

Ficino, M, *The Book of Life*, Tr. Charles Boer, Dallas, Texas, 1992

Field, JV, *Kepler's geometrical cosmology*, London, 1943, 1988

French, P, *John Dee*, London, 1987

Godwin, J, *Robert Fludd*, London, 1979

Godwin, J, *Harmonies of Heaven and Earth*, London, 1987

Godwin, J, *Music, Mysticism and Magic*, London, 1986

Gombrich, EH, *Symbolic Images. Studies in the Art of the Renaissance, with 170 Illustrations. II.*, Chicago, 1972, 1985

Greenhow, RC, *Introductory quantum mechanics*, Bristol, 1990

Gregory, John, *A Comparative View of the State & Faculties of Man with those of the Animal World*, London, 1765

Gregory, John, *Lectures on the Duties and Qualifications of a Physician*, London, 1772

Guthrie, WKC, *Orpheus and Greek religion*, London, 1935

Haller, JS Jnr, 'The Great Biological Problem: Vitalism, materialism, and the philosophy of organism', *New York State Journal of Medicine*, Vol.86, No.2, February 1986, pp. 81-88

Halliwell, S, *Plato: Republic 10*, Wiltshire, 1988

Hanslick, E, *On the Musically Beautiful*, Tr. Geoffrey Payzant, Indianapolis, 1986

Hanslick, E, *Vom Musikalisch-Schönen*, Leipzig, 1854

Heath, Sir Thomas L, *Aristarchus of Samos - the ancient Greek Copernicus*, Oxford, 1913

Heath, Sir Thomas L, *Greek Astronomy*, London, 1932; also New York 1991

Hegel, GWF, *Phenomenology of Spirit*, Tr. AV Miller, Oxford, 1977

Helmholtz, HLF, *Lehre von den Tonempfindungen* (2nd Ed.) 1885

Helmholtz, HLF, *On the Sensations of Tone*, Tr. AJ Ellis, New York, 1954

Huffman, CA, *Philolaus of Croton,* Cambridge, 1993

Huffman, WH, *Robert Fludd - essential readings*, London, 1992

Huffman, WH, *Robert Fludd and the end of the renaissance*, London, 1988

James, J, *The music of the spheres: music, science, and the natural order of the universe*, London, 1995

Jayne, SR, *Marsilio Ficino's commentary on Plato's Symposium*, Columbia, 1944 (Vol. 19 of University of Missouri Studies)

John von Neumann, *The Computer and the Brain*, London, 1958, 1974

Jung, CG & Pauli W, *The interpretation of nature and the psyche*, London, 1955

Kahn, CH, *Anaximander and the origins of Greek cosmology*, New York, 1960

Kassler, JC, *Inner Music: Hobbes, Hooke and North on Internal Character*, London, 1995

Kestrel, A, *The act of creation*, London, 1964

Kingsley, P, *Ancient philosophy, mystery and magic*, Oxford, 1995

Kirk, GS; Raven, JE; Schofield, M, *the pre-Socratic philosophers*, Cambridge, 1983

Kristeller, PO, *Eight philosophers of the Italian renaissance*, Stanford, 1966

Kristeller, PO, *The philosophy of Marsilio Ficino*, Tr. V Conant, Columbia, 1943

Kuhn, TS, *The structure of scientific revolutions*, Chicago & London, 1962, 1996

Langer, S, *Philosophy in a new key*, Camb. Mass. & London, 1942, 1993

Levin, FR, *The harmonics of Nicomachus and the Pythagorean tradition*, Pennsylvania, 1975

Lloyd, GER, *Polarity and Analogy - two types of argumentation in early Greek thought*, Cambridge, 1966

Lockwood, M, *Mind, Brain & the Quantum*, Oxford, 1992

Long, B, *The Origins of Man and the Universe*, London, 1984, 1998

Lovejoy, AO, *The Great Chain of Being*, Cambridge, Mass., 1936

Lowinsky, EE, 'Music in the culture of the renaissance', in Kristeller, PO & Wiener, PP, *Renaissance Essays*, New York, 1968, 1992

Mead, Richard, *The Medical Works of Richard Mead*, Edinburgh, 1792

Maula, E, 'The conquest of Time', *Diotima*, Vol.11, 1983, pp. 130-148

Melzer, SJ, 'Vitalism and Mechanism in Biology and Medicine', *Science*, Vol.XIX, No.470, 1904, pp. 18-22

Moyer, AE, *Musica Scientia*, Ithaca & London, 1992

Murray Barbour, J, *Tuning and Temperament*, New York (originally Michigan), 1951, 1972

Myers, CS, 'Vitalism: A Brief Historical and Critical Review', *Mind*, Vol.9, 1900, pp. 218-233; 319-331

O'Neal, *Early astronomy from Babylonia to Copernicus*, Sydney, 1986

Pagels, H, *The Cosmic Code*, London, 1982

Pauli, W, 'The influence of archetypal ideas on the scientific theories of Kepler', in CG Jung & Pauli W, *The interpretation of nature and the psyche*, London, 1955

Penrose, Roger, *Shadows of the Mind*, Oxford, 1994

Penrose, Roger, *The Emperor's New Mind*, Oxford, 1989

Philip, JA, *Pythagoras and early Pythagoreanism*, Toronto, 1966

Plato, *The Republic*, Tr. D Lee, London, 1955, 1987

Plato, *The Symposium*, Tr Walter Hamilton, London, 1951

Plato, *Timaeus and Critias*, Tr. D Lee, 1965, 1977

Plato, *The Last Days of Socrates*, Tr. H Tredennick and H Tarrant, London, 1954, 1993

Porter, R, 'Medical lecturing in Georgian London', *British Journal for the History of Science*, 1995, 28, pp. 91-99

Rattansi, PM, 'Art and Science: The Paracelsian Vision', in *Science and the Arts in the Renaissance*, Ed. JW Shirley & FD Hoeniger, London & Toronto, 1985, pp. 50-58

Reedy, J, *Thomas Norton's Ordinal of Alchemy*, Oxford, 1975

Richardson, H, 'The Myth of Er (Plato, *Republic*, 616B)', *CQ*, 20, 1926

Robinson, B, Robinson, Bryan, *A treatise of the animal eoconomy*, Dublin, 1732

Schavernoch, H, *Die Harmonie der Sphären*, Munich, 1981

Schopenhauer, A, Tr. EFJ Payne, *The world as will and representation*, New York, 1958, 1969

Scott, W (Tr), *Hermetica*, (1924), Bath, 1992

Shorey, P, *Platonism Ancient and Modern*, Berkeley, 1938

Solomon, J, *Harmony in Ptolemy's Harmonics*, Armindale, NSW, 1990

St. John of the Cross, *Living Flame of Love*, Tr. EA Peers, Tunbridge Wells, 1935, 1987

Stewart, JA, *The Myths of Plato*, London, 1960

Stoullig, C, 'Symbols and forms' in Bertrand, Pascale (Ed.), *Brancusi*, Paris, 1995

Sutton, G, 'The Physical and Chemical Path to Vitalism: Xavier Bichat's *Physiological researches on Life and Death*', *Bulletin of the History of Medicine*, Vol.58, Spring 1984, No.1, pp. 53-71

Tarnas, R, *The Passion of the Western Mind*, London, 1991

Taub, LC, *Ptolemy's universe*, Chicago & LaSalle, Illinois, 1993

Taylor, AE, *A Commentary on Plato's Timaeus*, Oxford, 1928

Taylor, T, *Iamblichus on the mysteries of the Egyptians, Chaldeans, and Assyrians*, London, 1821

Taylor, T, *The works of Plato*, London, 1804

Tillyard, EMW, *The Elizabethan World Picture*, London, 1943, 1972

Von Neumann, J, *The Computer and the Brain*, London, 1958

Walker, DP, *studies in musical science in the late renaissance*, London, 1978

Wigner, EP, 'Remarks on the mind-body question', in Good, IJ (Ed.), *The Scientist Speculates: An Anthology of Partly Baked Ideas*, London, 1962

Wittgenstein, *Tractatus Logico-Philosophicus*, Tr. CK Ogden, London, 1922, 1981

Yates, FA, *Giordano Bruno and the Hermetic Tradition*, Chicago, London & Toronto, 1964

www.ingramcontent.com/pod-product-compliance
Lightning Source LLC
La Vergne TN
LVHW051350080426
835509LV00020BA/3368